Ottawa Ontario Book 4 in Colour Photos, Saving Our History One Photo at a Time

Photography
by Barbara Raué
2016

Series Name:
Cruising Ontario

Book 149: Ottawa Book 4

Cover photo: Murray Street, Page 50

Series Name: Cruising Ontario
Saving Our History One Photo at a Time
in colour photos

Books Available in Alphabetical Order:
Aberfoyle, Acton, Alton, Amherstburg, Ancaster, Arthur, Aylmer, Ayr, Bloomingdale, Brantford, Burlington, Caledon, Caledonia, Cambridge, Clifford, Conestogo, Delhi, Dorchester to Aylmer, Drayton, Drumbo, Dundas, Eden Mills, Elmira, Elora, Essex, Fergus, Guelph, Hagersville, Hamilton, Hanover, Harriston, Hespeler, Jarvis, Kingston, Kingsville, Kitchener, Linwood, Listowel, London, Lucknow, Mono, Mount Forest, Neustadt, New Hamburg, Niagara-on-the-Lake, Oakville, Orangeville, Orillia, Owen Sound, Palmerston, Peterborough, Petrolia, Port Elgin, Preston, Rockwood, Sarnia, Seaforth, Sheffield, Shelburne, Simcoe, Southampton, St. Jacobs, St. Marys, St. Thomas, Stoney Creek, Stratford, Thamesford, Tillsonburg, Waterdown, Waterford, Waterloo, Welland, Wellesley, Windsor, Wingham, Woodstock

Book 123-124: Kingsville
Book 125-127: Woodstock
Book 128: Thamesford
Book 129-132: St. Marys
Book 133-136: Sarnia
Book 137: Petrolia
Book 138-139: Welland
Book 140-145: Kingston
Book 146-149: Ottawa

Other Books by Barbara Raue

Coins of Gold

Arrows, Indians and Love

The Life and Times of Barbara
Volume 1: Inventions That Have Enhanced My Life
Volume 2: Entertainment That I Have Enjoyed
Volume 3: East Coast Trips
Volume 4: Olympics Have Always Intrigued Me
Volume 5: Wonders of the World
Volume 6: Caribbean Cruises We Have Enjoyed
Volume 7: Animals
Volume 8: Storms and Other Major Disasters in My Lifetime
Volume 9: Wars, Terrorist Attacks and Major Disasters

The Cromwell Family Book

Laura Secord Discovered

Daddy Where Are You?

Montana Series
Book 1: Montana Dream
Book 2: Life on the Montana Frontier
Book 3: Montana to Boston and Back

Visit Barbara's website to view all of her books
http://barbararaue.ca

Table of Contents

The ByWard Market has been the heart of Ottawa's commercial activities since the early 19th century. Throughout its history it has been a market for farmers in the Ottawa region and associated with wholesale and retail purchase of natural products and trade of manufactured goods and supplies. It has provided the services and sometimes the industrial support to consolidate the markets role as the center of Ottawa commerce.

The heart of the market is characterized by low profile buildings typical of the nineteenth century interspersed with succeeding commercial development until the 1970s. Its development pattern is extremely dense, covering full and sometimes multiple lots in many areas. Much of the land has been developed and redeveloped to provide services and support to its vital commerce. Secondary space in this area has traditionally been used for a variety of residential, storage and office facilities. In form, the architecture is diverse and layered, having been renovated, renewed and reformed frequently to adjust to changing commercial needs and priorities.

Pictures begin on Page 7.

Lowertown West comprises the City's oldest residential area. It was the civilian center of Ottawa from the British survey of the town site in 1826 until the turn of the 20th century. From about 1890 to the mid-1970s growth occurred in other areas of the city at the expense of Lowertown and much of the urban fabric east of King Edward and north of Boteler was demolished during urban renewal.

The Lowertown West Heritage Conservation District encompasses the area of Lowertown west of King Edward Avenue and east of Sussex Avenue between Bolton and St. Patrick Streets. In this book, buildings on Guigues, Parent and St. Patrick Streets are included. Lowertown includes early institutional buildings, including the Basilica and the Elizabeth Bruyére Centre, and a rich collection of residential buildings that demonstrate the early history of Lowertown and its gradual evolution. This evolution is a crucial characteristic of the area, and it recognizes the heritage value of buildings constructed over a long period of time. The history of Lowertown West is also the history of generations of Ottawa's working people, both French and English speaking, and the physical record of that social history, represented by both the institutions and the residential buildings, is a major cultural resource for the City of Ottawa.

Pictures begin on Page 33.

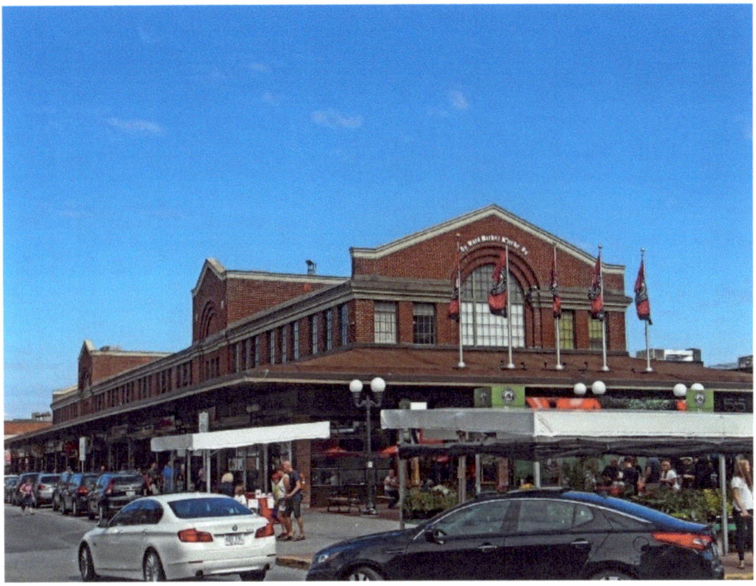

Jacobean Gables

By Ward Market - 1927

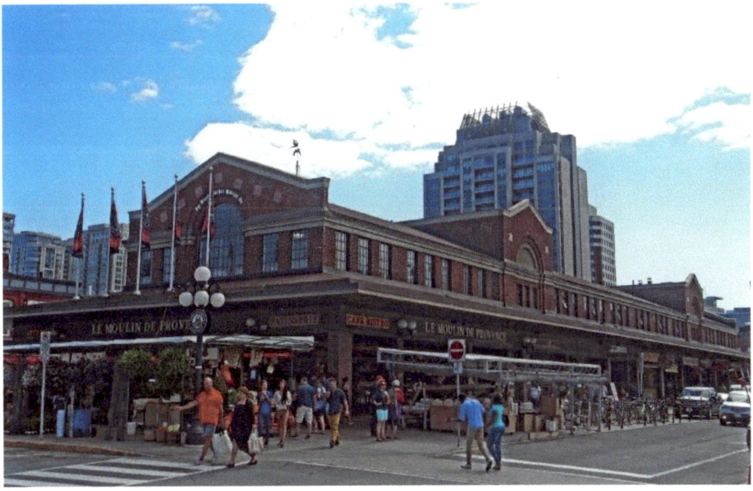

55 Byward Market Square - Le Moulin de Provence

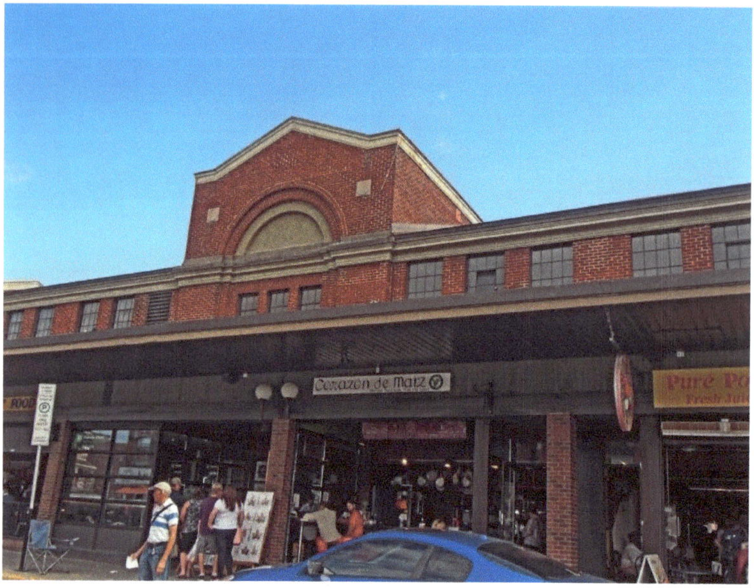

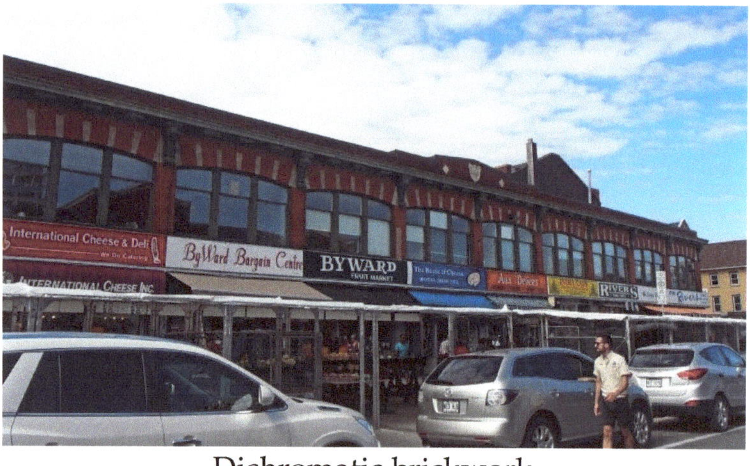

Dichromatic brickwork

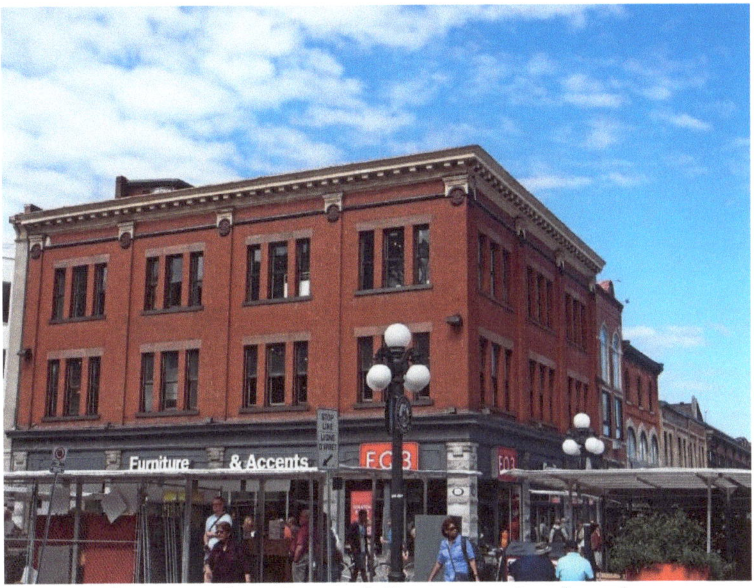

Pilasters, dentil moulding, cornice brackets

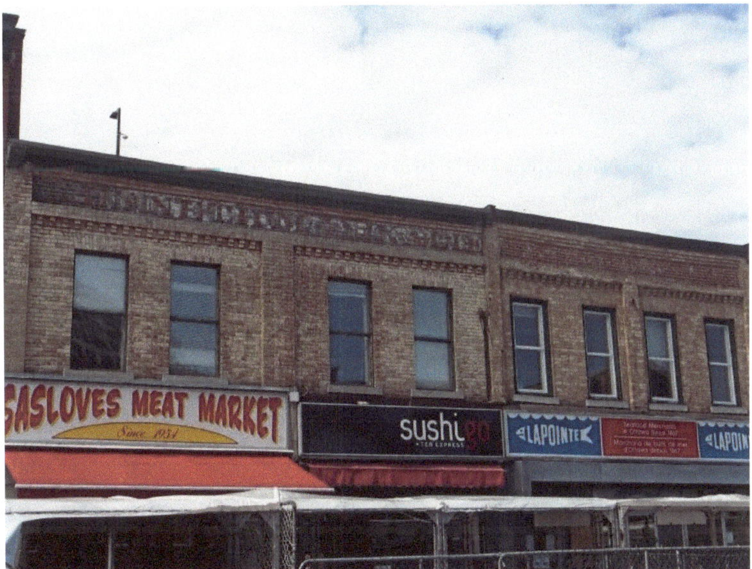

50 Byward Market - dentil moulding

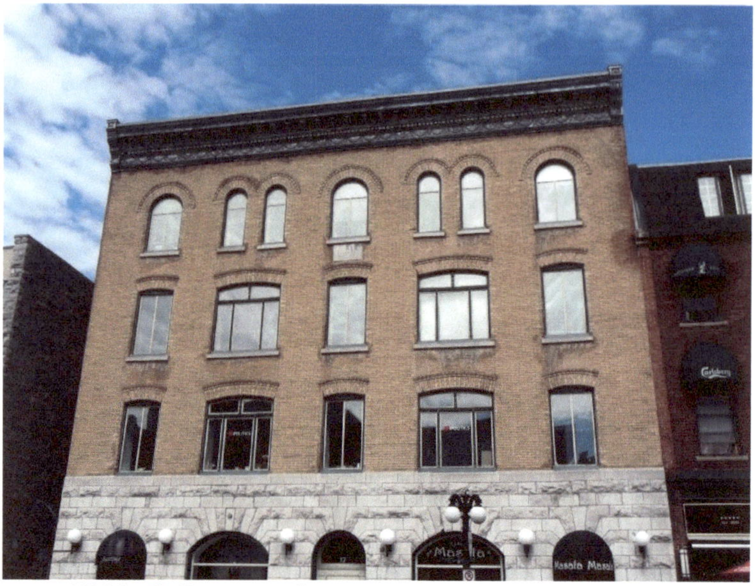

17 York Street - decorative cornice, voussoirs

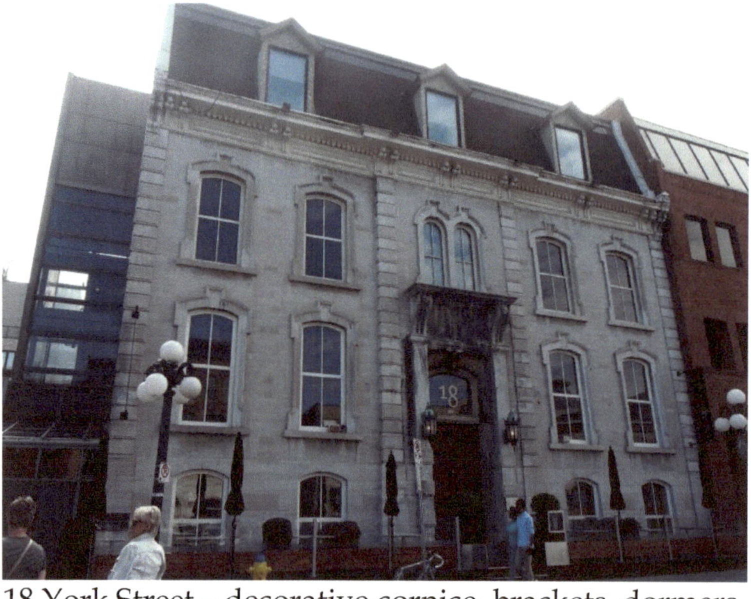

18 York Street - decorative cornice, brackets, dormers, keystones above windows, quoins

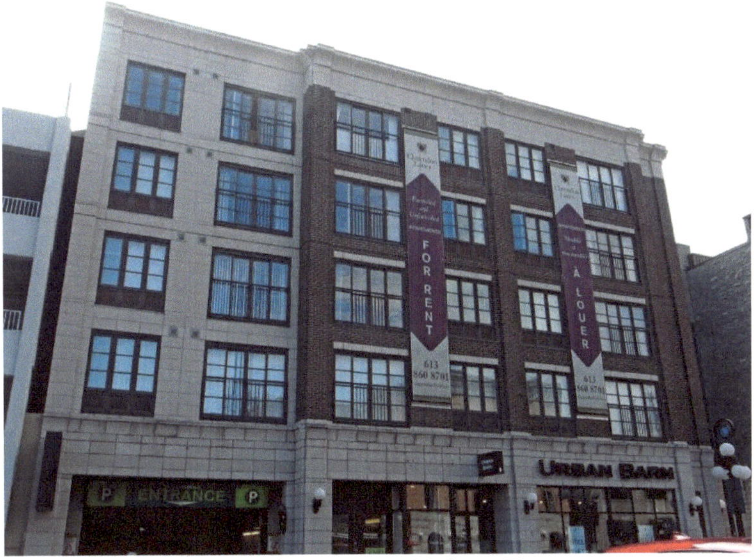

22 York Street – Urban Barn

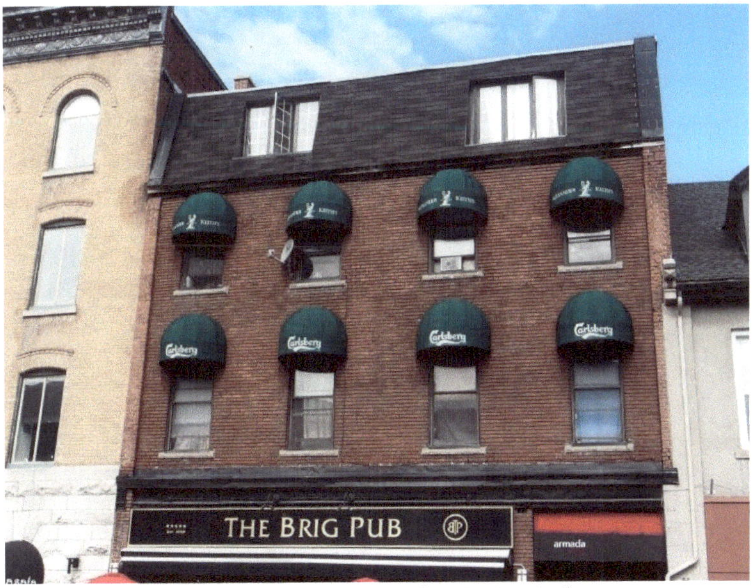

23 York Street – The Brig Pub

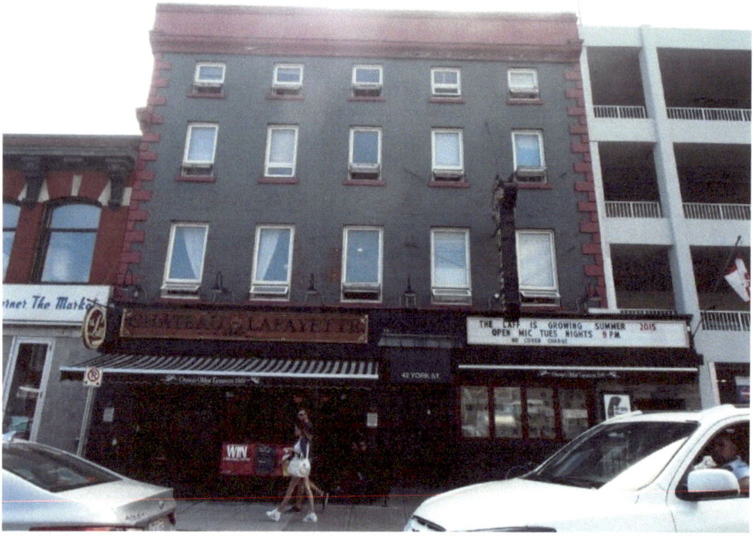

42 York Street - Chateau Lafayette, Canada's oldest tavern - established 1849 - corner quoins

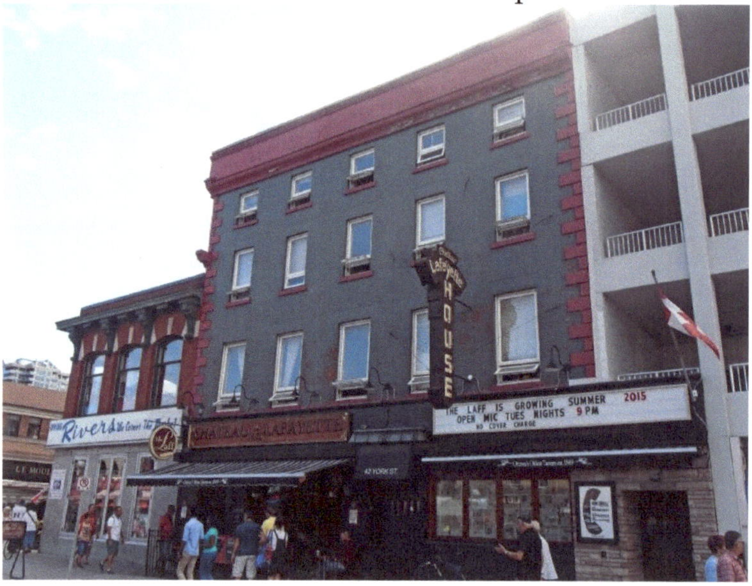

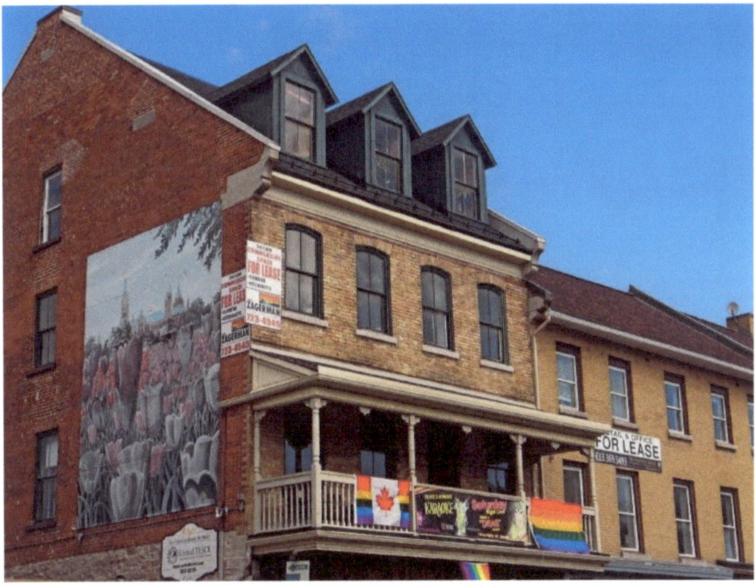

41 York Street - Kinki Bar - dormers in attic

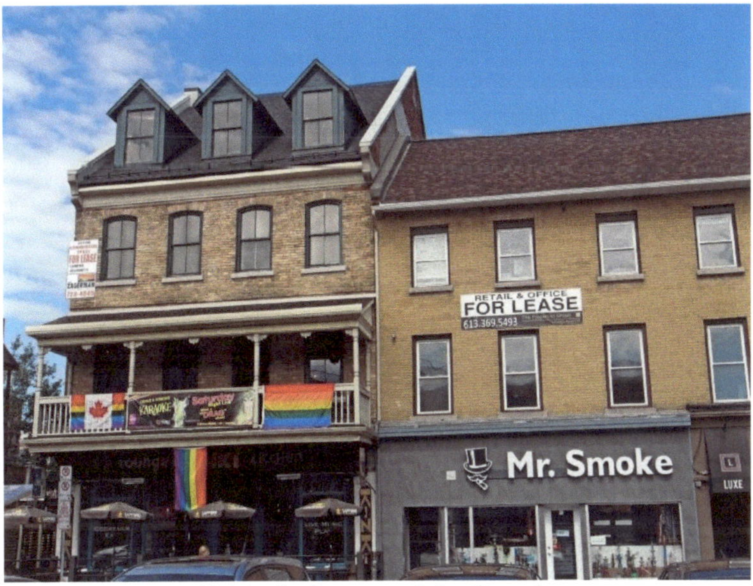

43 York Street - Mr. Smoke

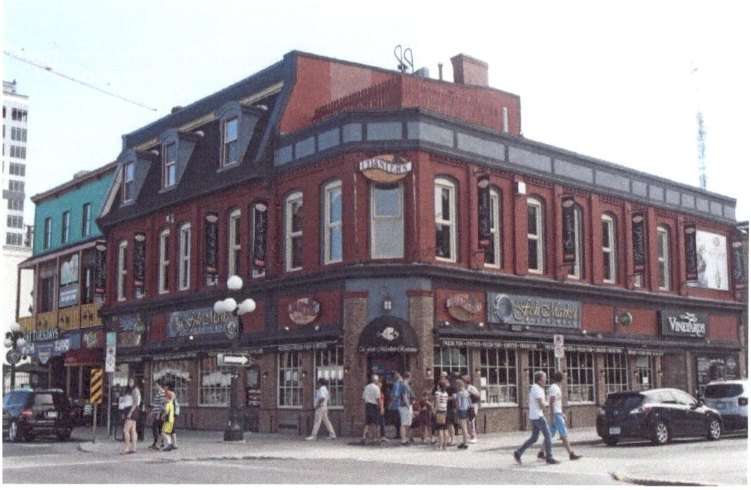

54-60 York Street – Swalwell-Borbridge Building – 1875 - The Fish Market Restaurant - dormers, dentil moulding

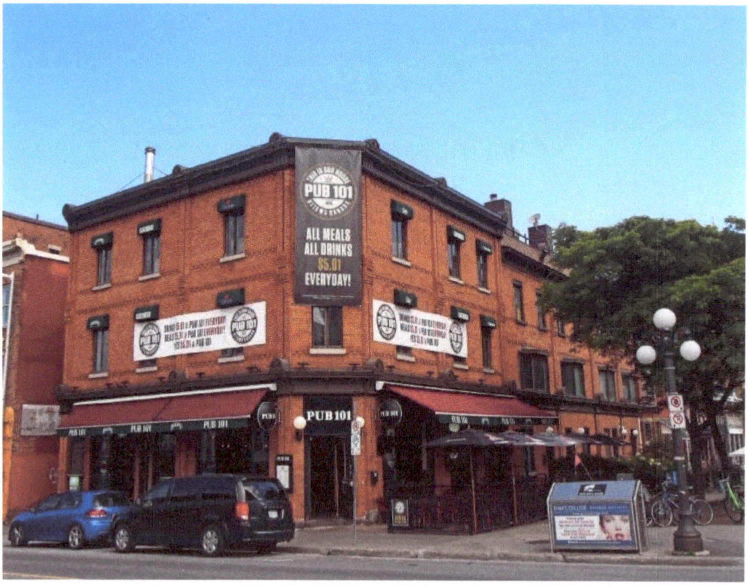

101 York Street – Pub 101 - dentil moulding, pilasters

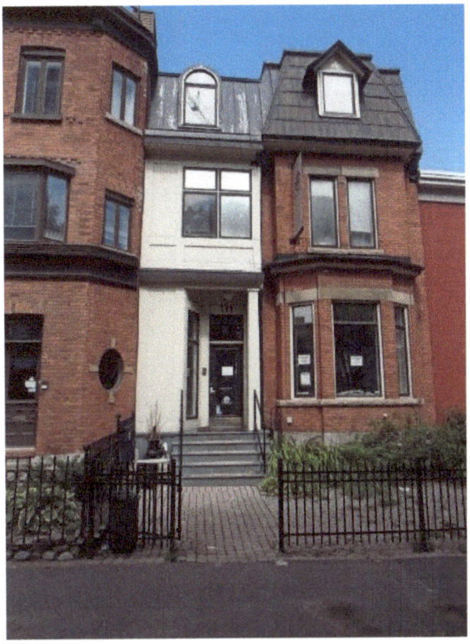

111 York Street
Bay window, dormers

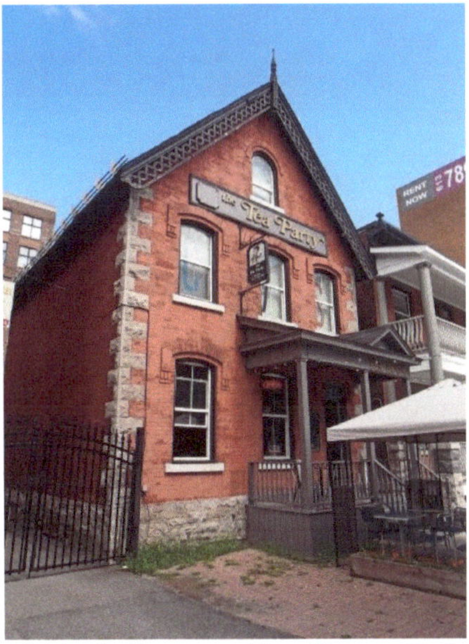

119 York Street – Tea Party Cafe
corner quoin, verge board
on gable with finial

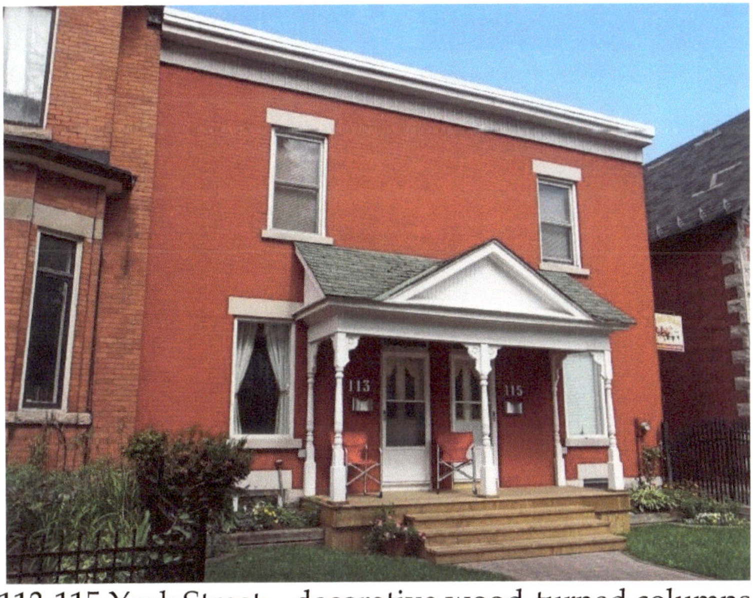

113-115 York Street – decorative wood-turned columns, pediment

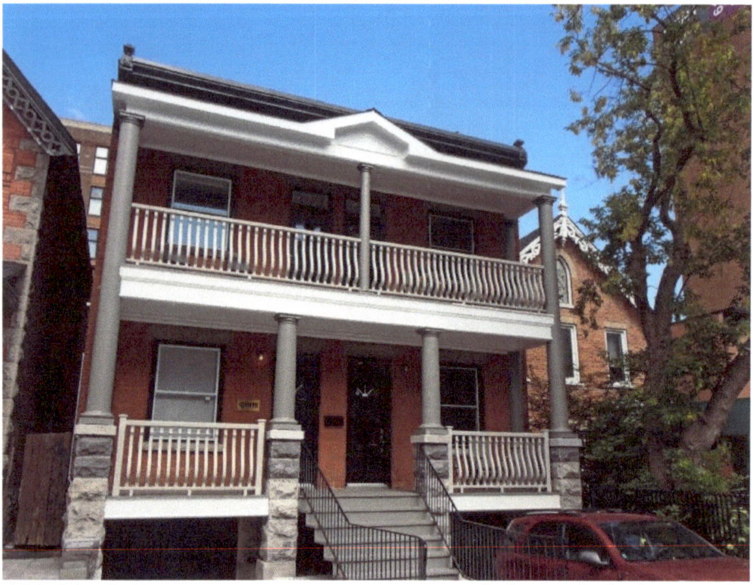

123 York Street - two-storey verandah with balustrade

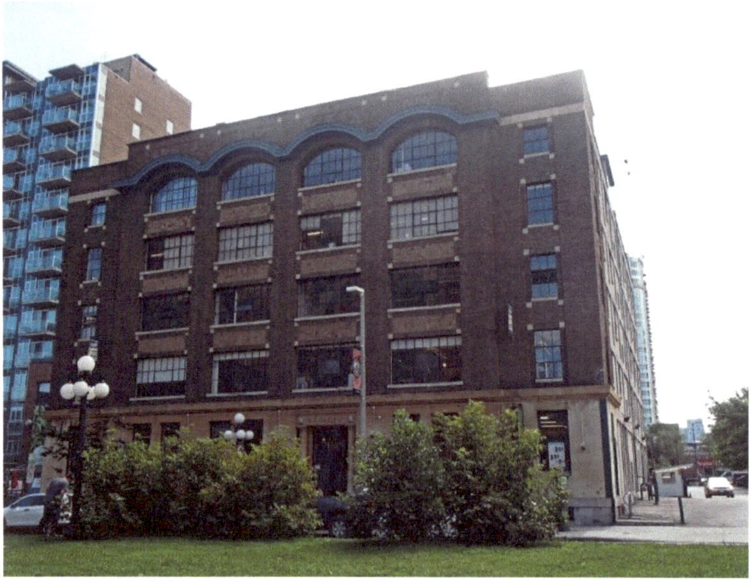

126 York Street – S. J. Major Limited

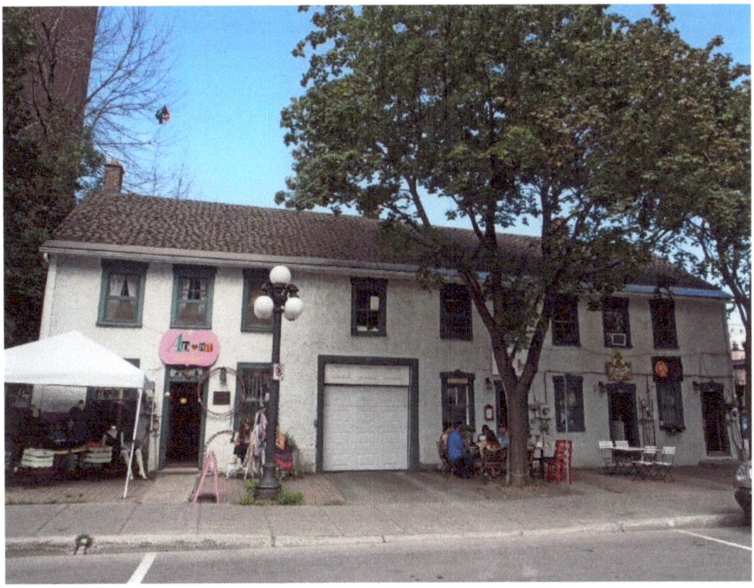

153-161 York Street - Brown Tenements – 1875 – built for Archibald Brown, a hotel keeper

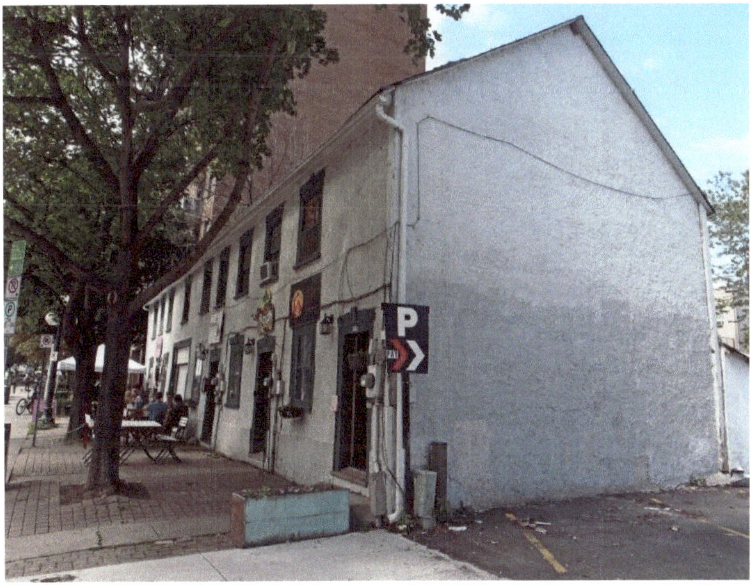

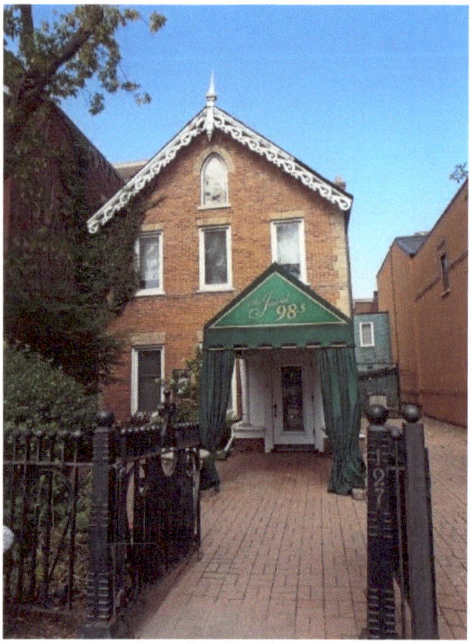

127 York Street - verge board trim and finial on gable
Gothic

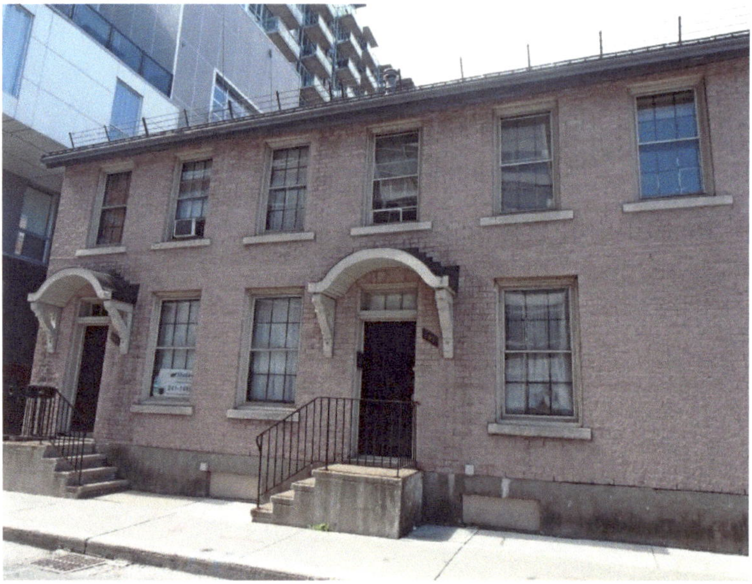

350-352 Cumberland Street – c. 1860 - hoods above doors, multi-paned windows

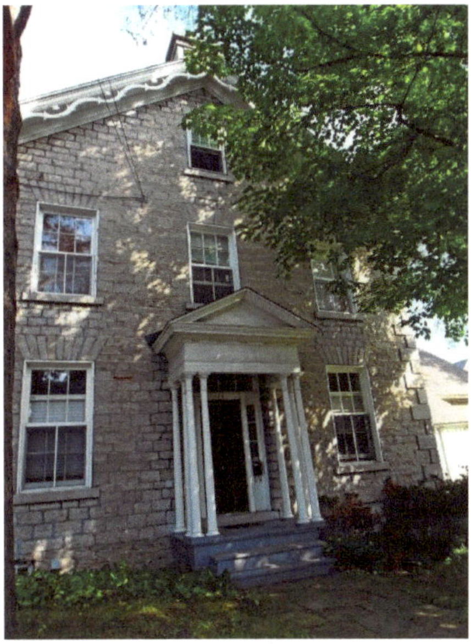

71 Thomas Street - verge board trim, pediment
Gothic

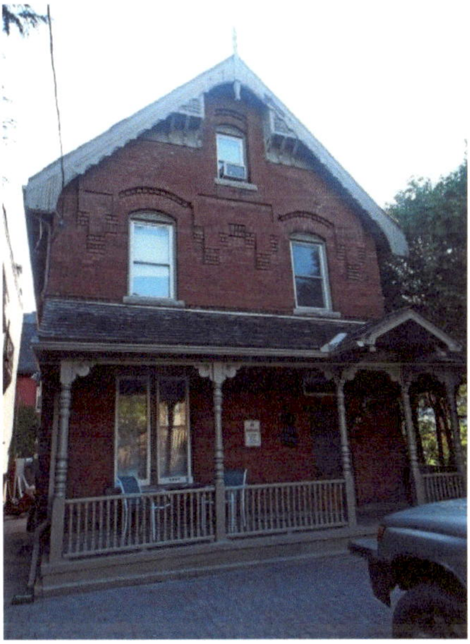

62 Somerset Street East - 1895 - built for Sarah and Andrew Mitrow - Gothic - verge board trim and finial

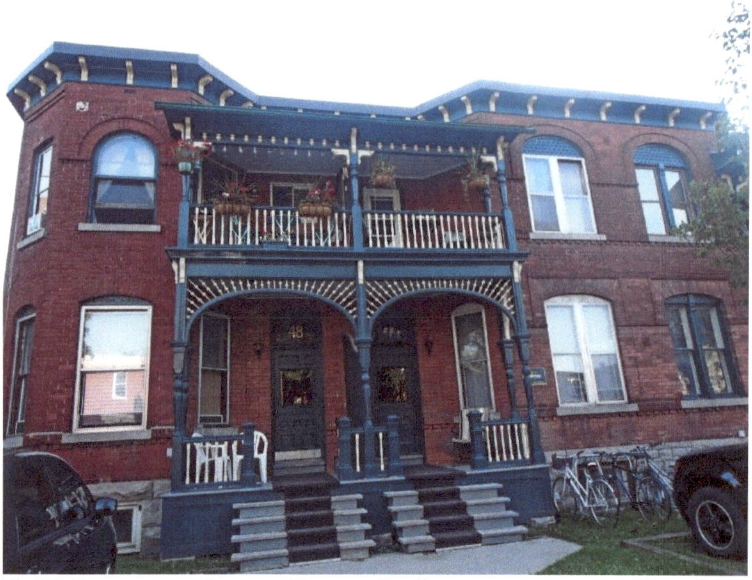

46-48 Somerset Street East – Italianate - cornice brackets; tower-like bay; wood-turned columns with decorative spindles

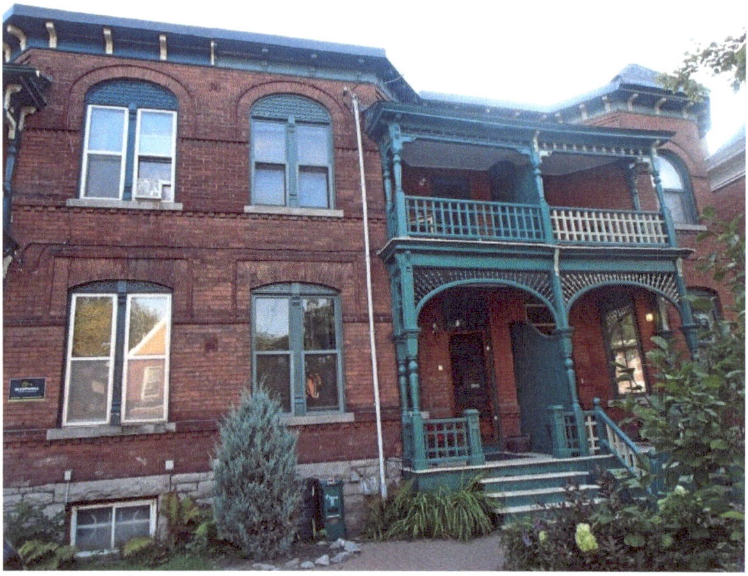

Somerset Street East – Italianate - cornice brackets; open railing on porch and balconies

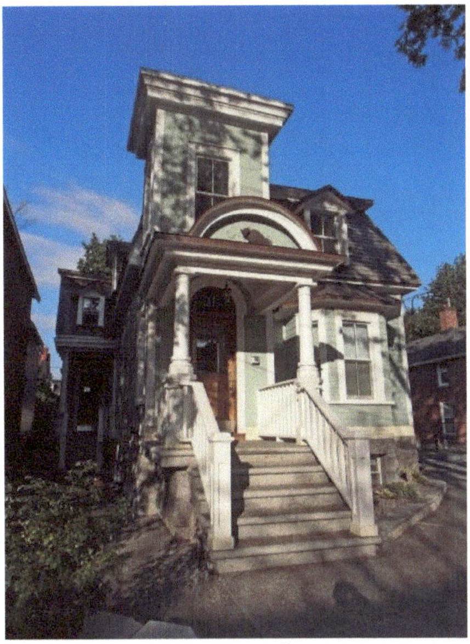

31 Somerset Street East – tower, dormers, circular pediment, bay window - Victorian

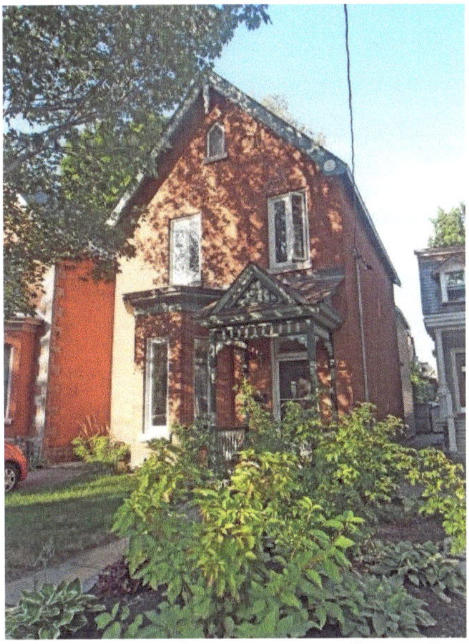

Somerset Street East – Gothic – verge board trim with finial, pediment

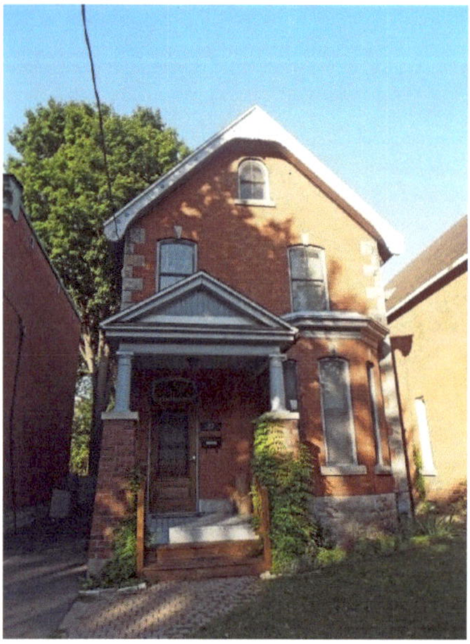

27 Somerset Street East - Gothic - pediment, bay window

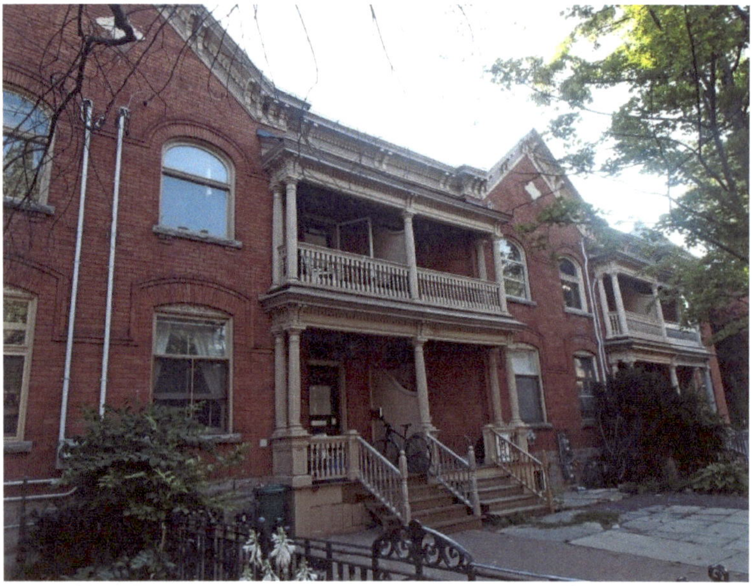

28-30 Somerset Street East - cornice brackets

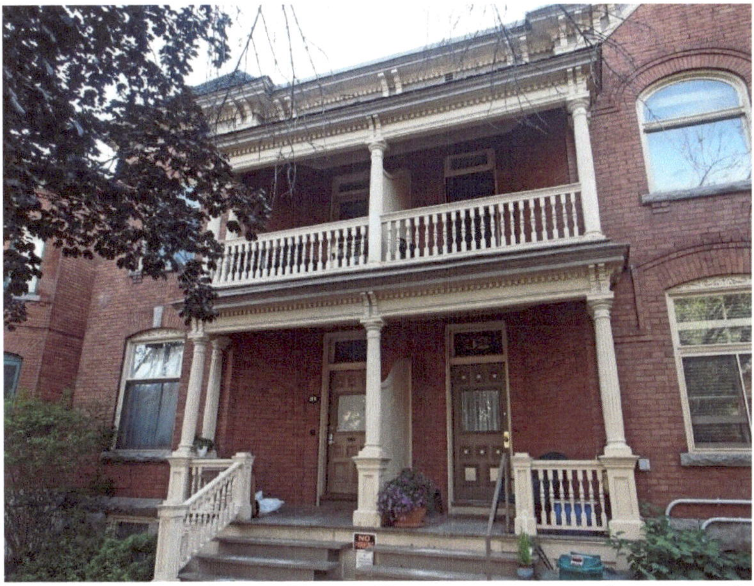

32-34 Somerset Street East – Romanesque style voussoirs

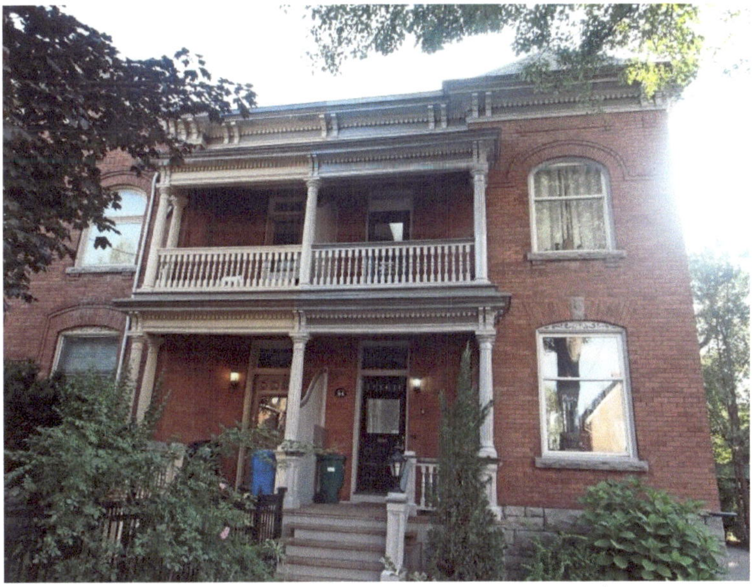

24-26 Somerset Street East - Romanesque style voussoirs

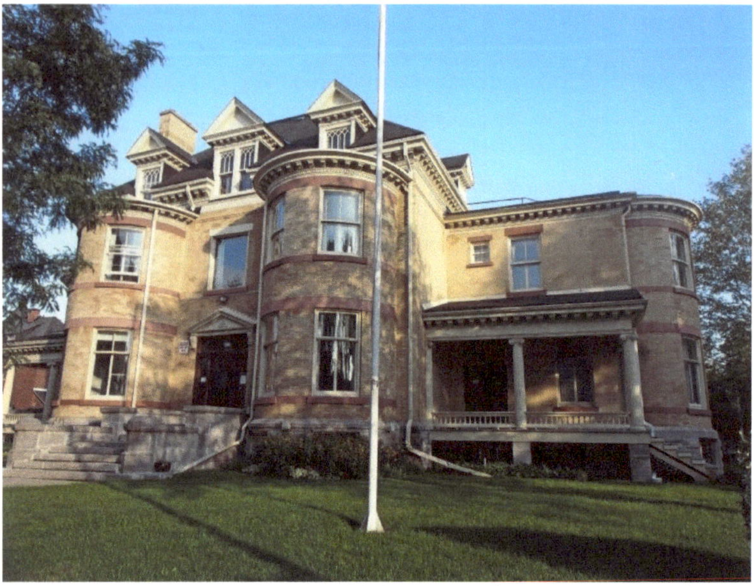

312 Laurier Avenue East - 1900 - Goodwin House - built for George Goodwin, Railway contractor - one of the largest Victorian mansions built in Ottawa
Two-storey towers, dormers, banding, pediment above door, Ionic capitals on porch supports, open railing

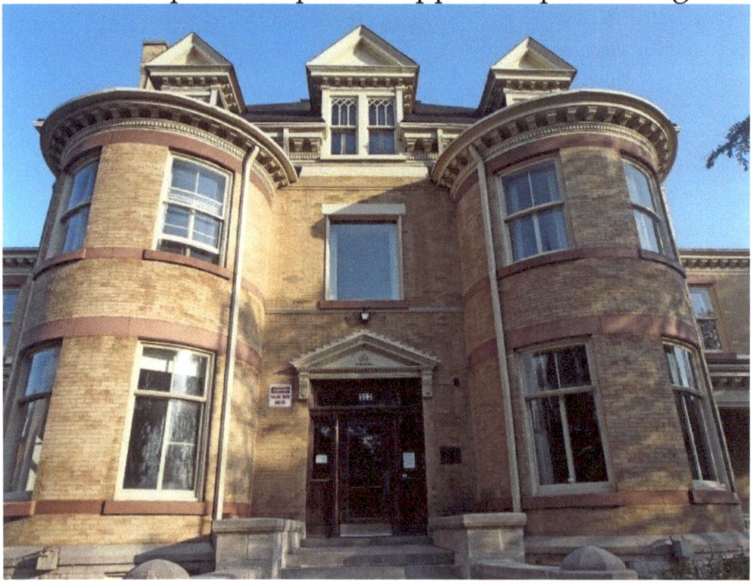

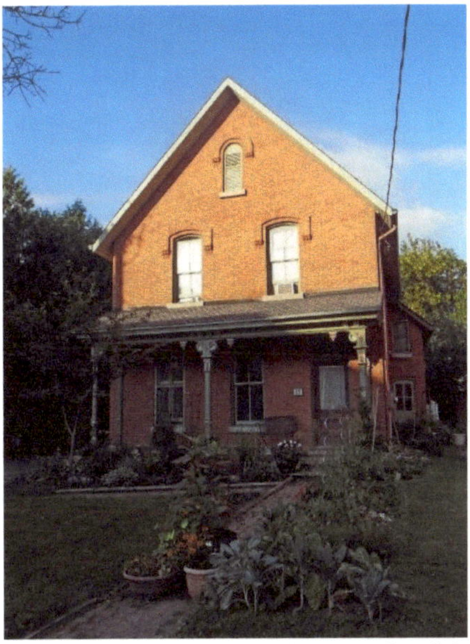

17 Somerset Street East - Gothic

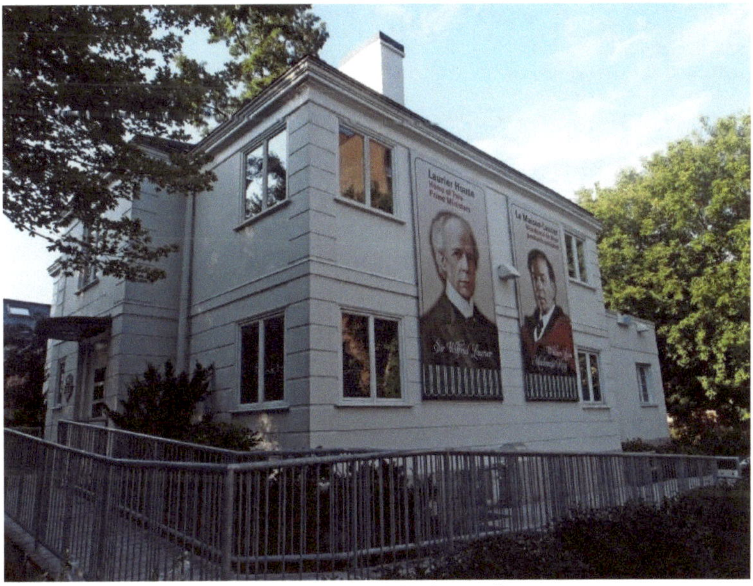

Laurier House Visitor Centre

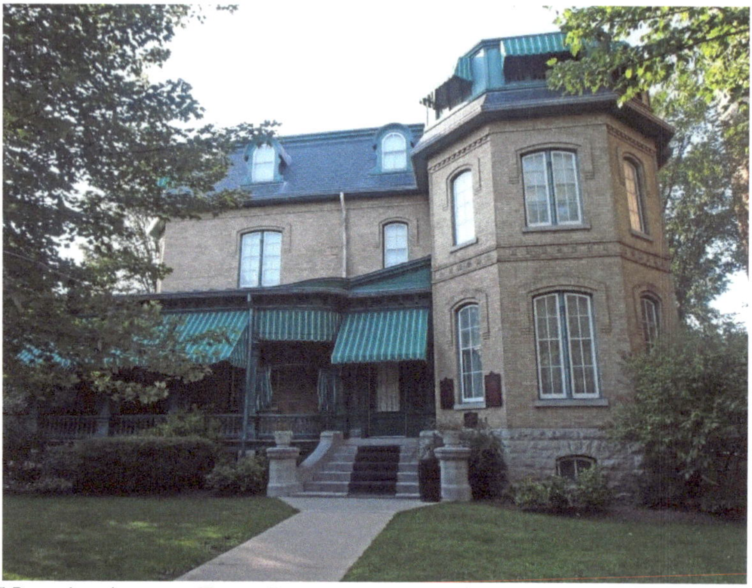

335 Laurier Avenue East - Laurier House – home of Prime Ministers Sir Wilfrid Laurier and William Lyon Mackenzie King – Victorian mansion built in 1878 – Second Empire/Italianate - Many distinguished guests were received at this house, such as King George VI, Sir Winston Churchill, Charles de Gaulle, and Franklin D. Roosevelt.

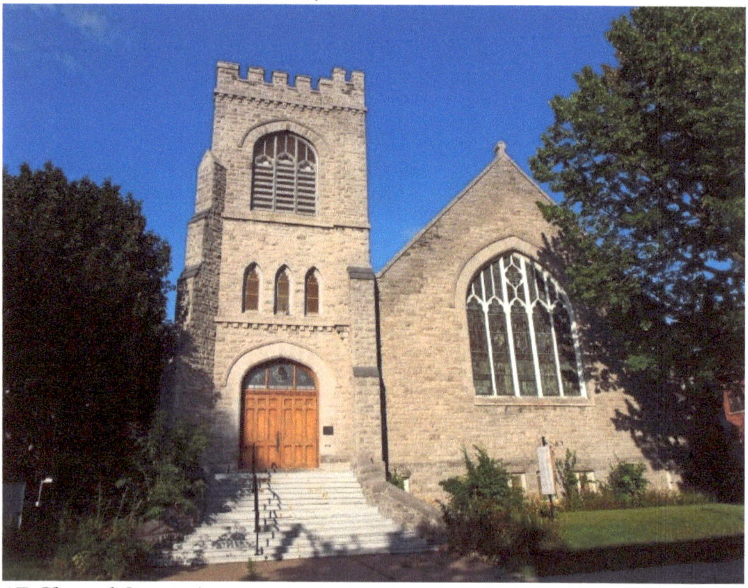

317 Chapel Street (at Laurier) - All Saints Anglican Church – Gothic Revival – 1900 – stained glass windows, crenellated tower, lancet windows

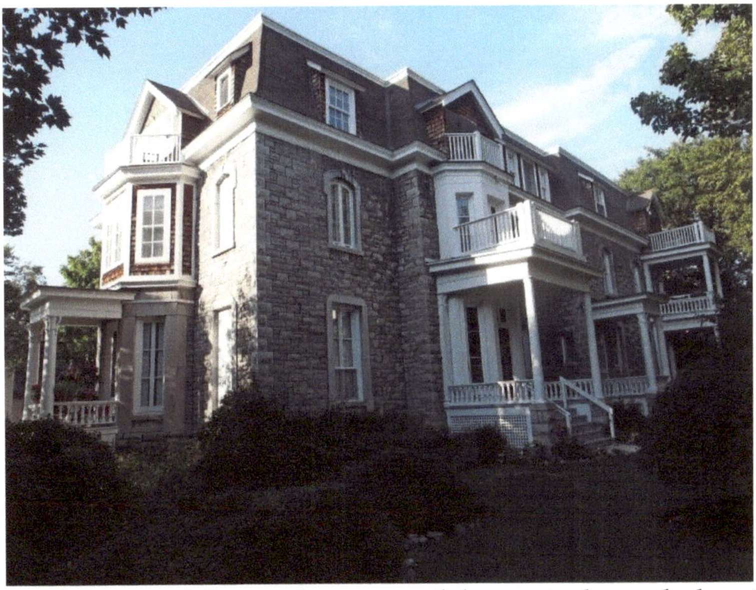

Chapel Street - Mansard-type roof, bay windows, balconies

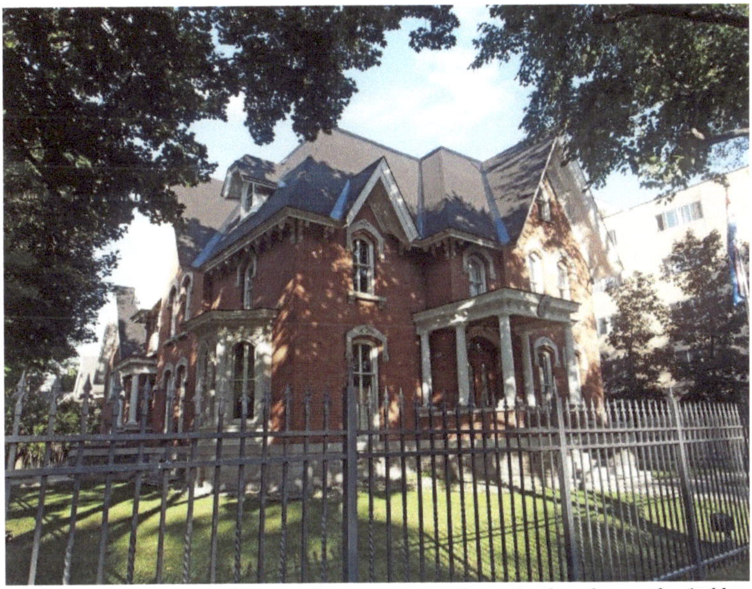

229 Chapel Street - Victorian - steeply pitched roof, different sized gables, cornice brackets, decorative window and door surrounds, bay windows, Doric pillars on verandah

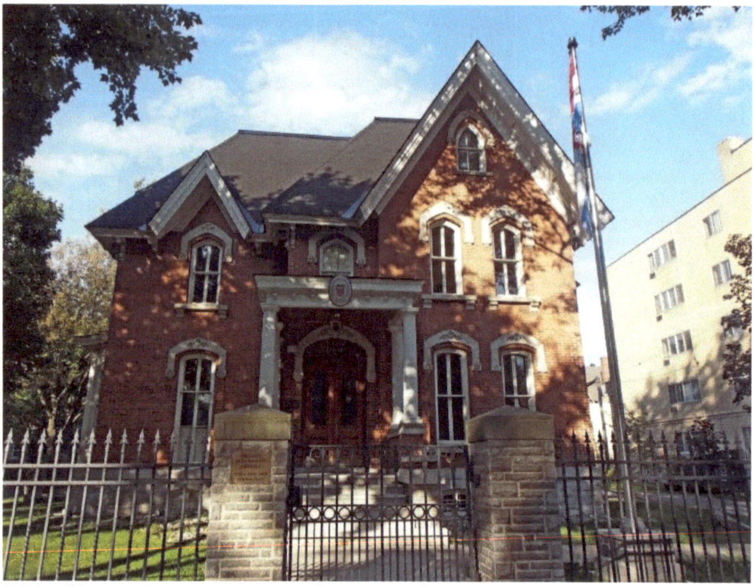

229 Chapel Street - Embassy of the Republic of Croatia

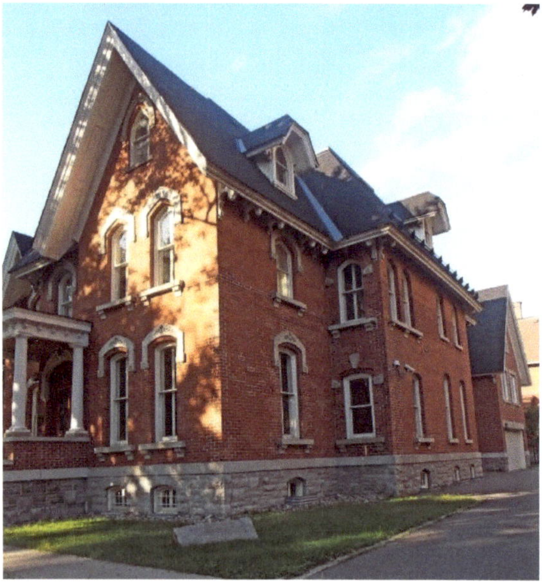

229 Chapel Street - dormers

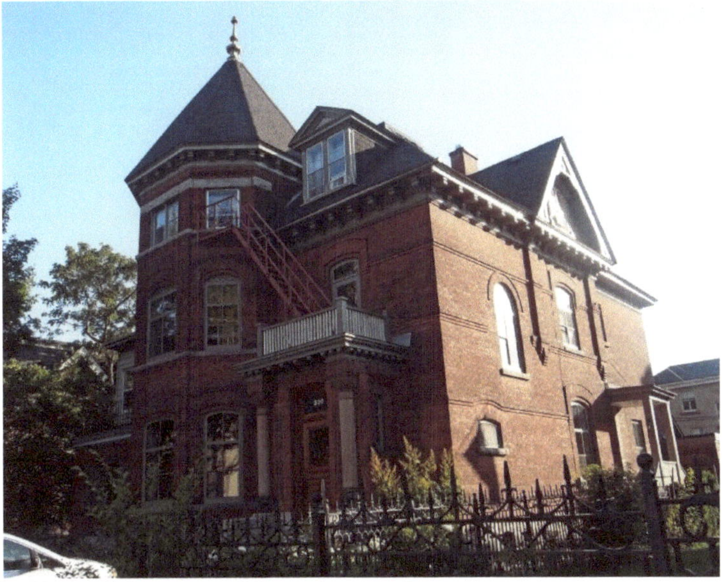

320 Chapel Street - Victorian - three-storey tower, cornice brackets, gable, voussoirs, banding

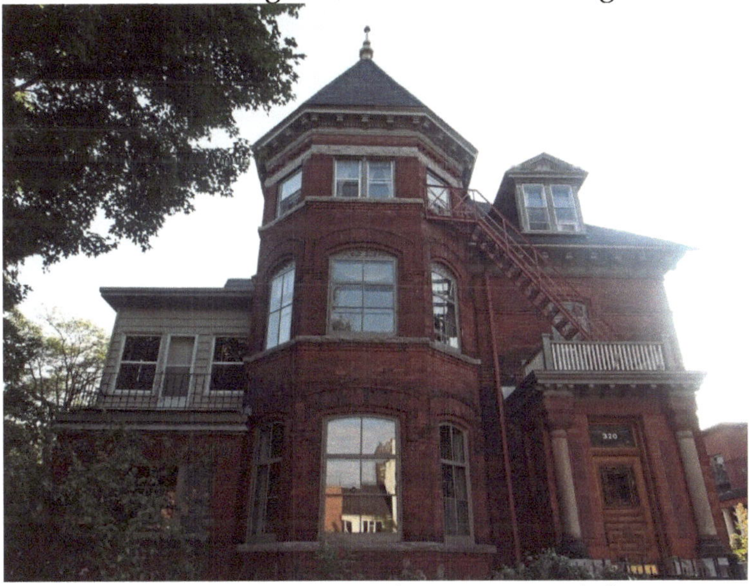

Dormer, composite columns around door

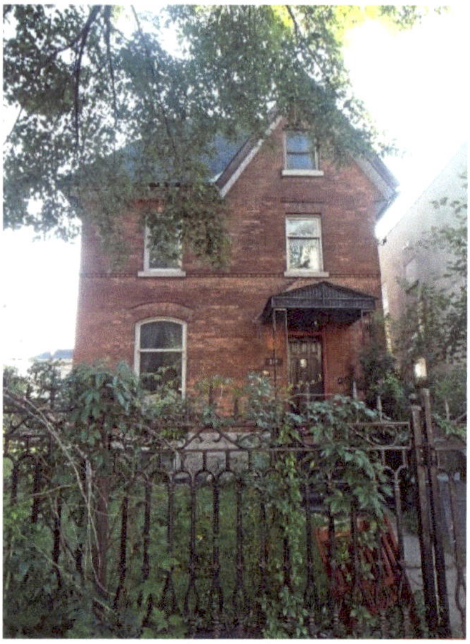

312 Chapel Street

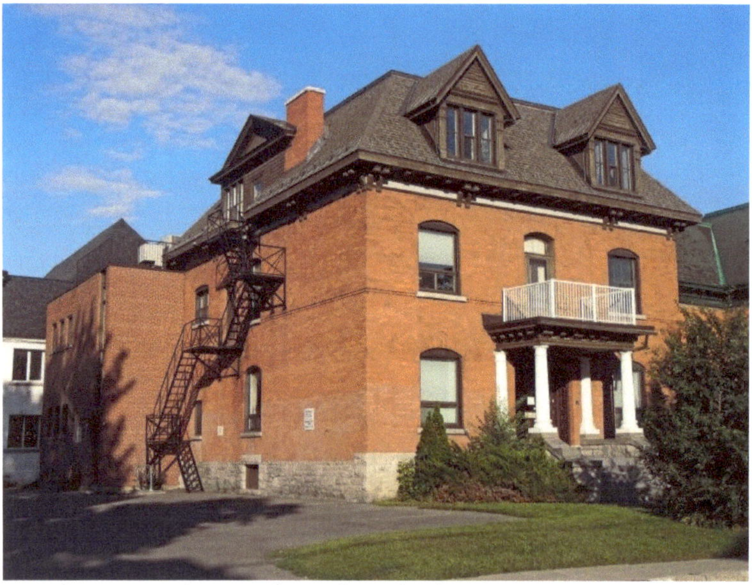

Italianate - hipped roof with dormers, Doric pillars supporting porch roof with balcony above

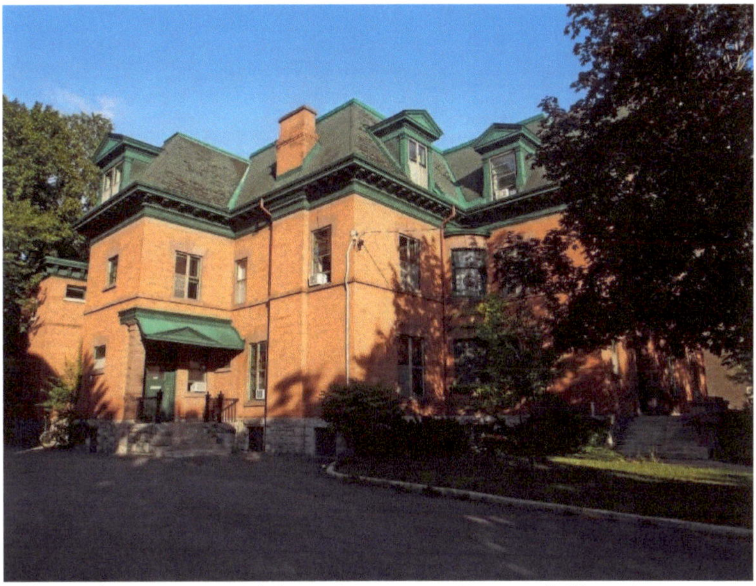

323 Chapel Street - Kildare House - Second Empire, mansard roof, dormers

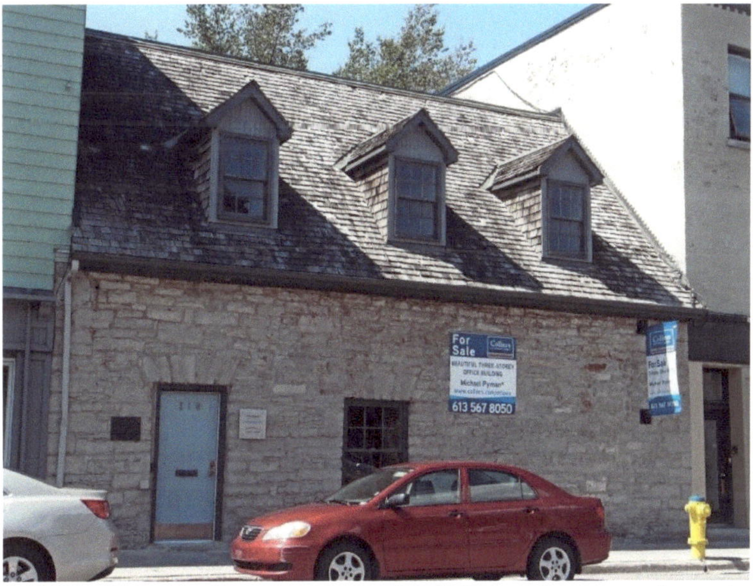

210 Dalhousie Street - stone building, dormers in attic

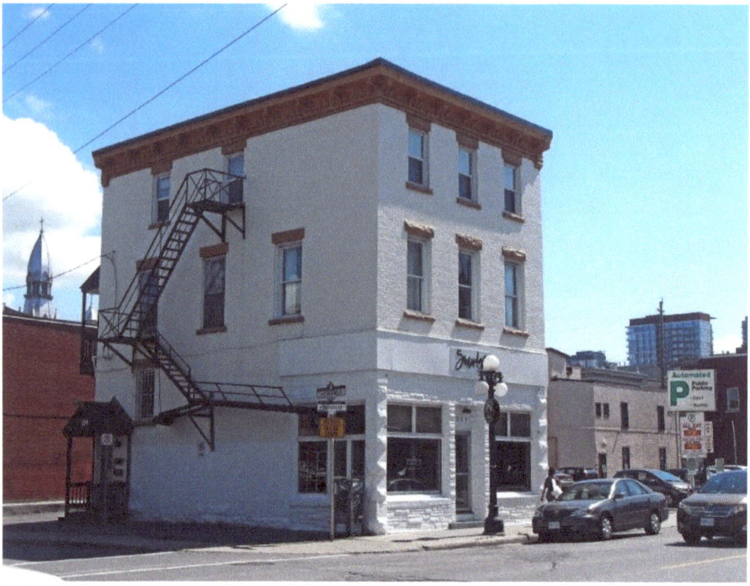

223 Dalhousie Street - cornice brackets, decorative cornice, dentil moulding

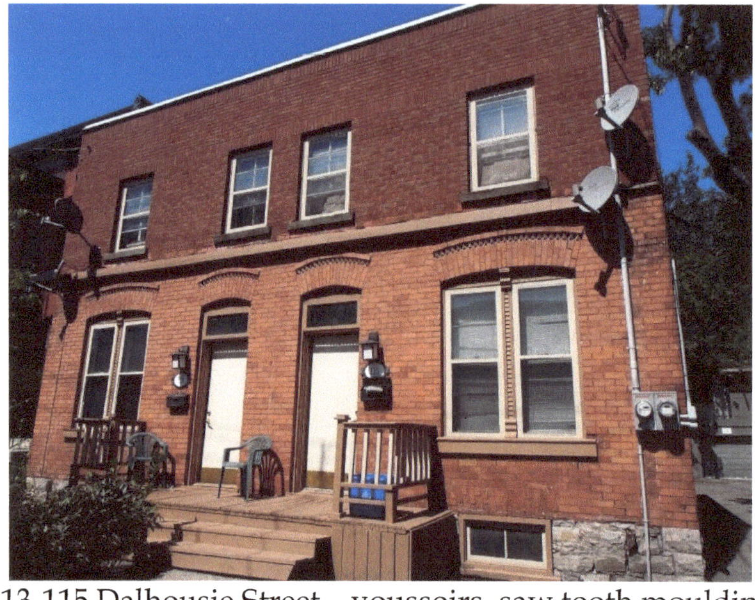

113-115 Dalhousie Street - voussoirs, saw tooth moulding

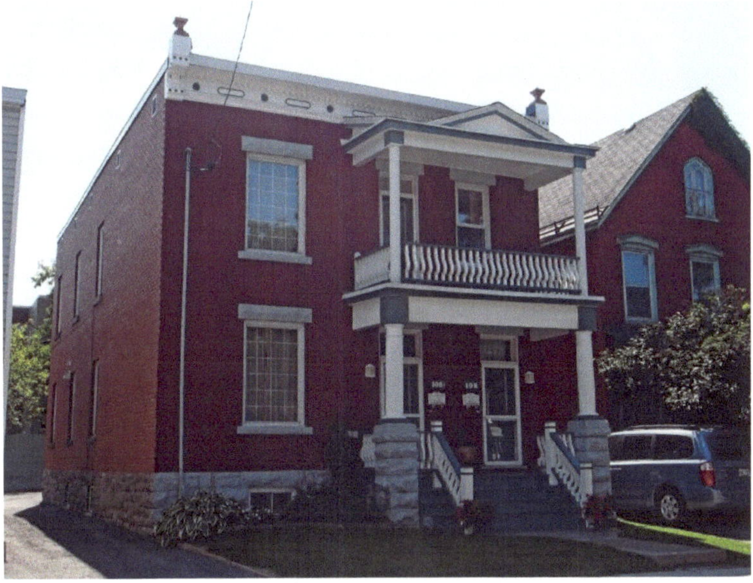

108 Dalhousie Street – decorative cornice, two-storey porch topped with pediment

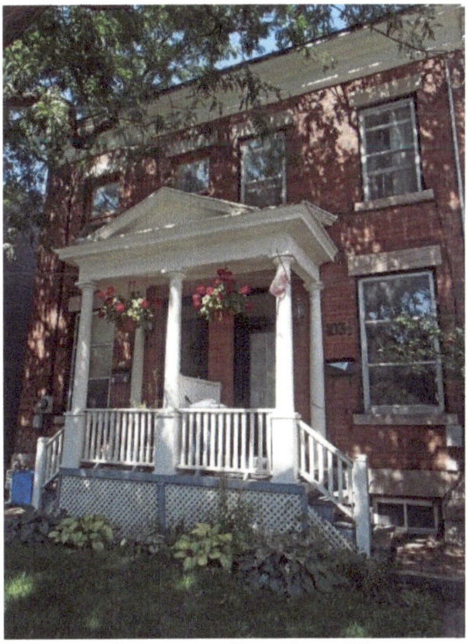

103 Dalhousie Street – Doric pillars, pediment

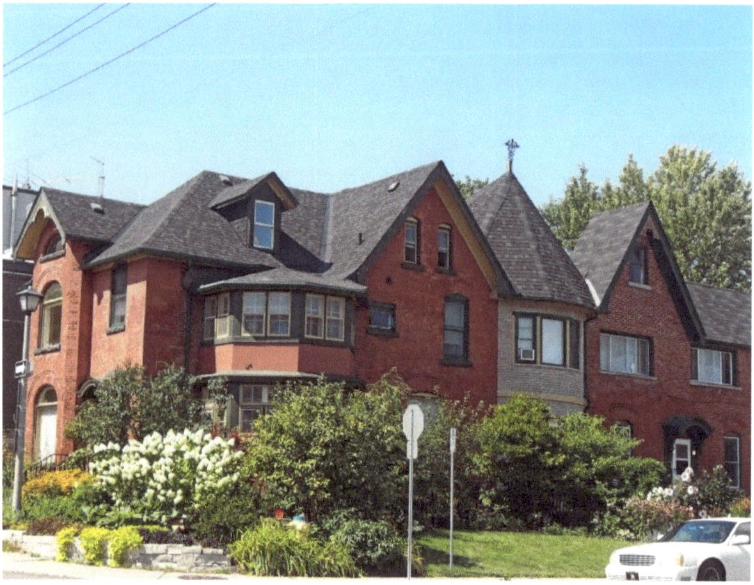

Dalhousie Street - Victorian - two-storey tower-like bay with dormer above, plus turret with cone-shaped roof

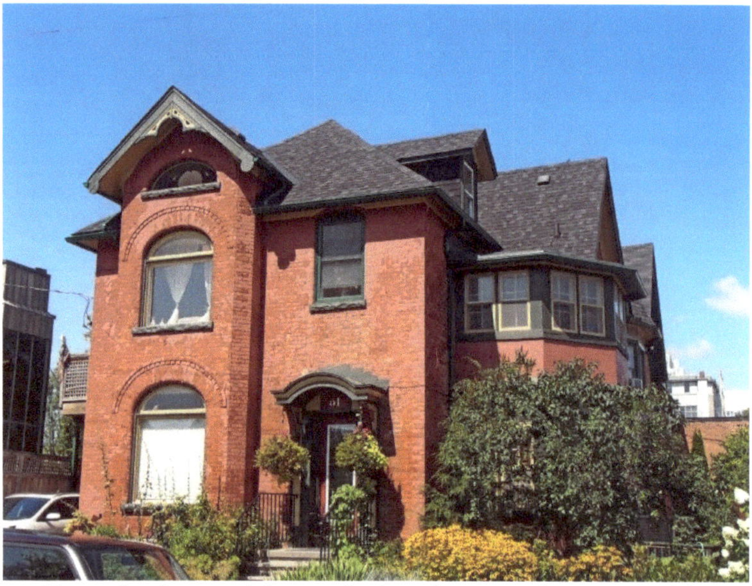

Frontispiece with semi-circular window in gable

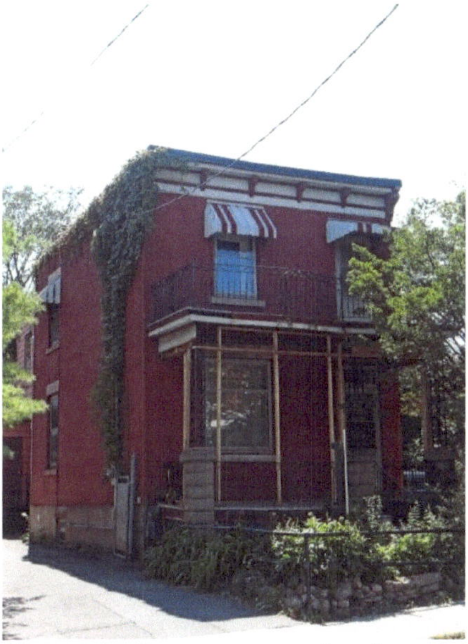

Dalhousie Street – cornice brackets

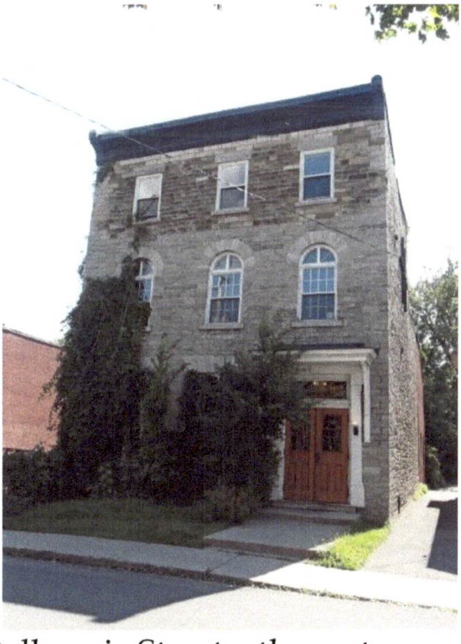

90 Dalhousie Street – three-storey stone

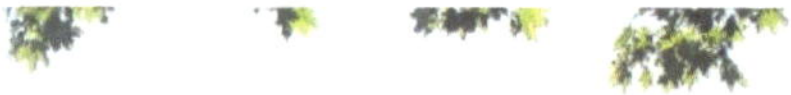

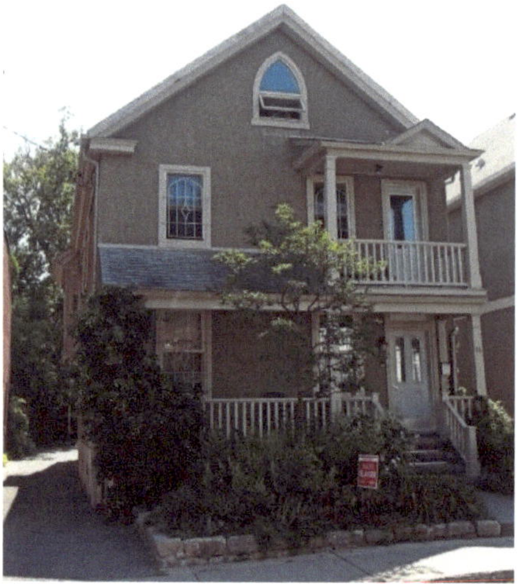

88 Dalhousie Street - cornice return on gable, second-floor balcony with pediment

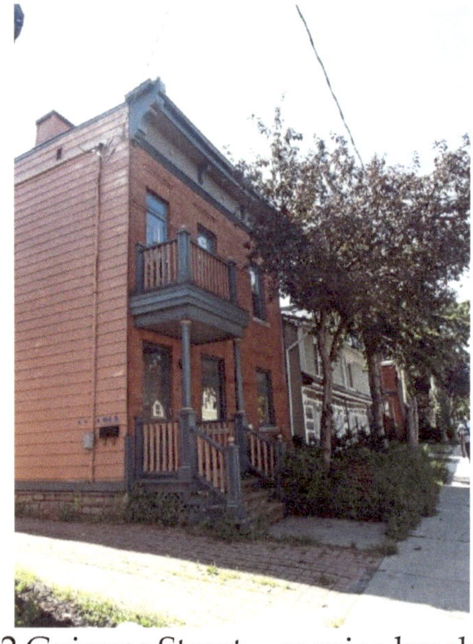

162 Guigues Street - cornice brackets

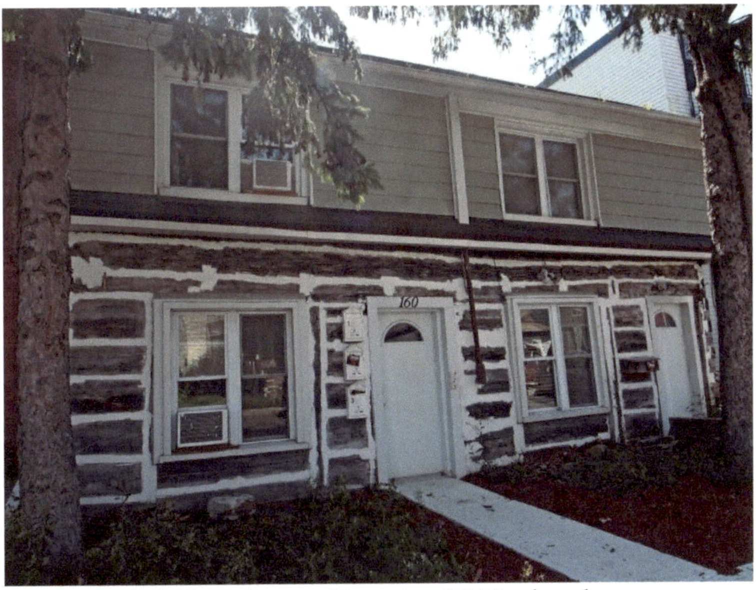

158-160 Guigues Street – 1846 - log house

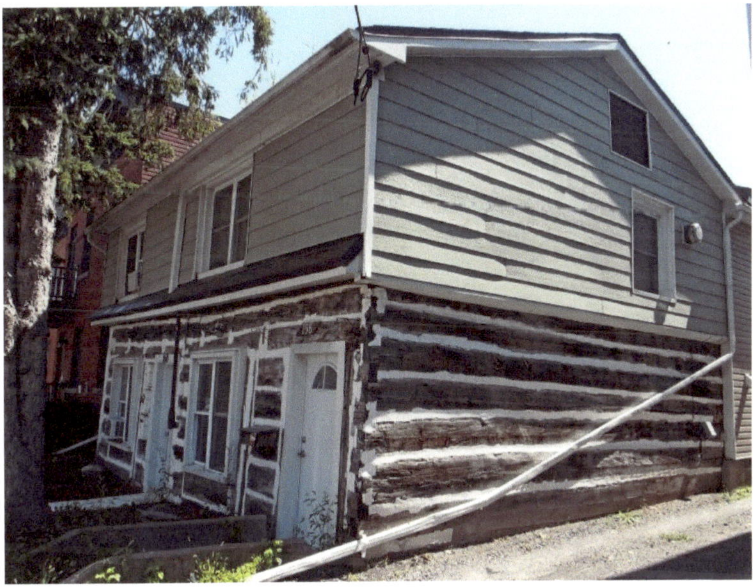

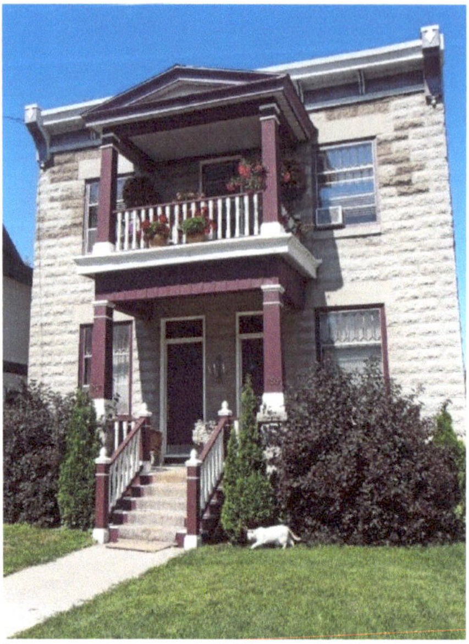

159 Guigues Street - second floor balcony with pediment

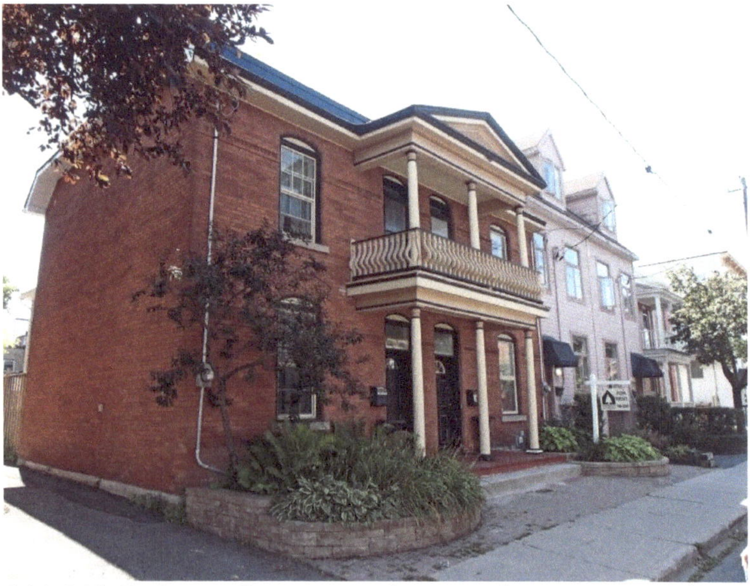

146-148 Guigues Street - pediment above second-floor balcony

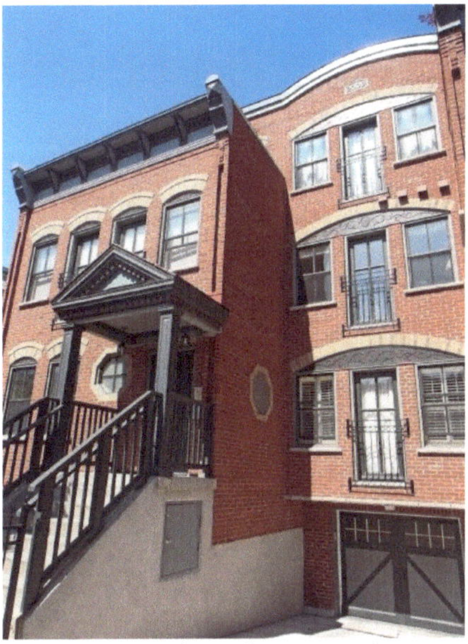

Guigues Street - cornice brackets, pediment above porch

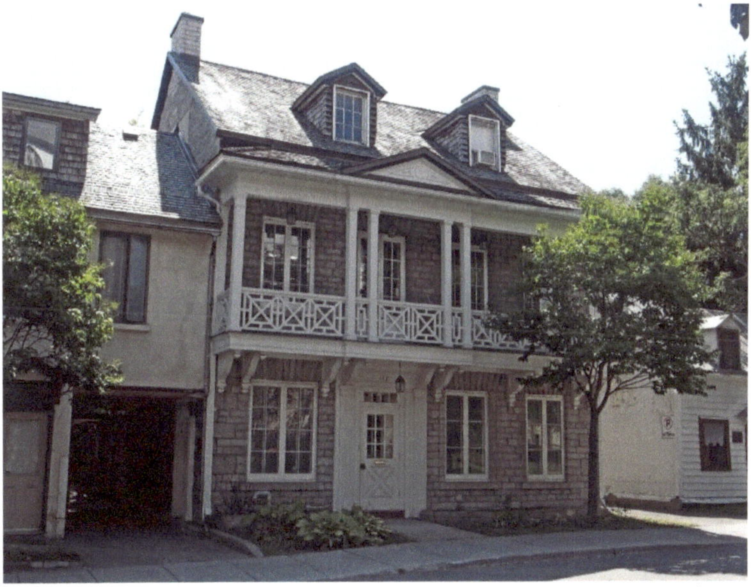

142 Parent Avenue - dormers; pediment over centre of second floor balcony; cornice brackets below to support balcony; multi-light transom window above door

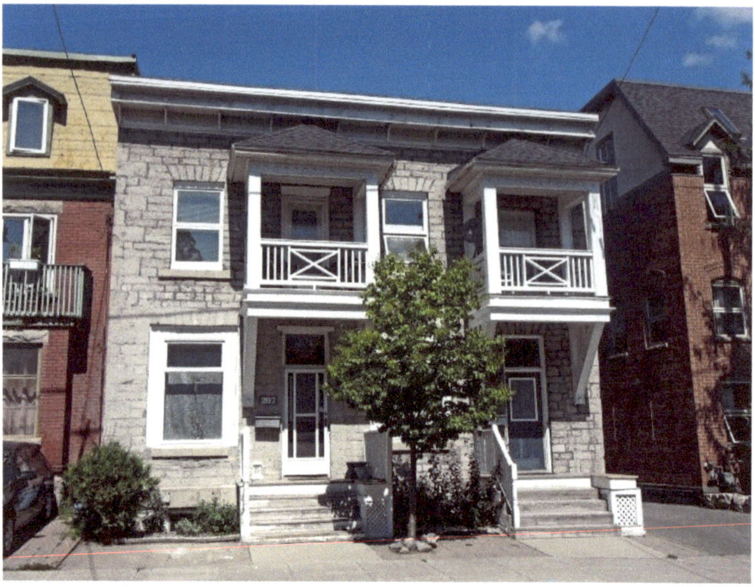

207 St. Patrick Street - pediments above second floor balconies

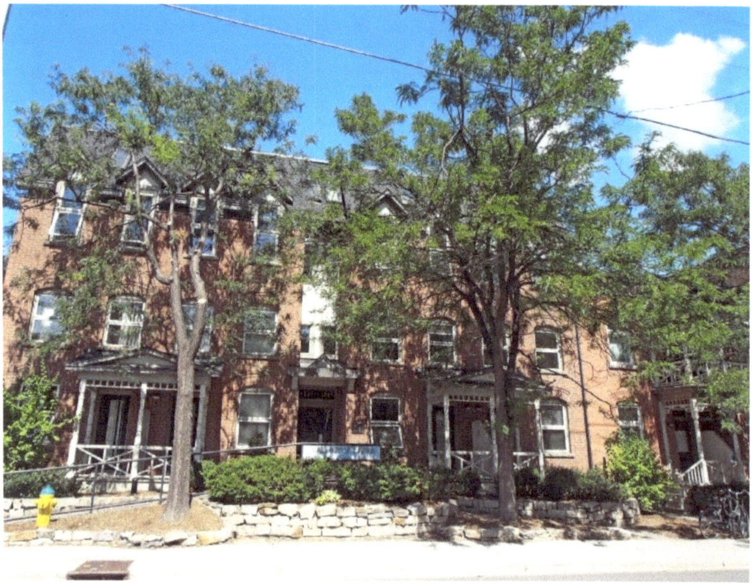

215 St. Patrick Street

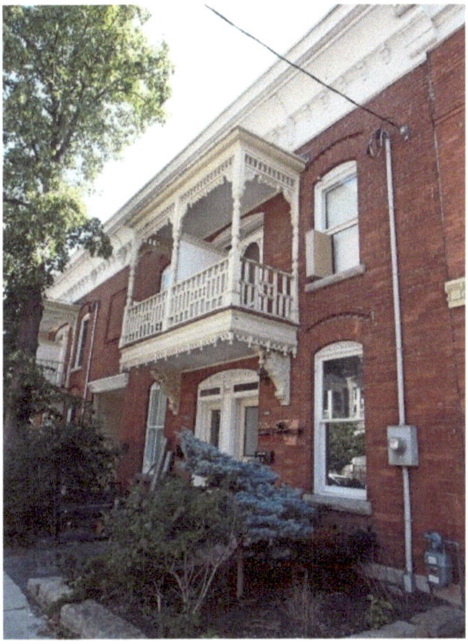

204-210 St. Patrick Street – Brousseau Terrace - 1898

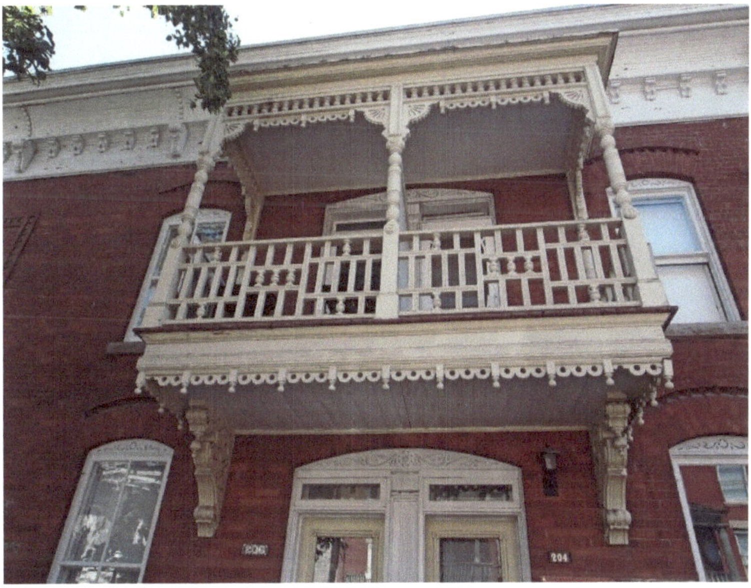

Sleeping porch – decorative brackets supporting balcony with decorative wood-turned supports, open railing

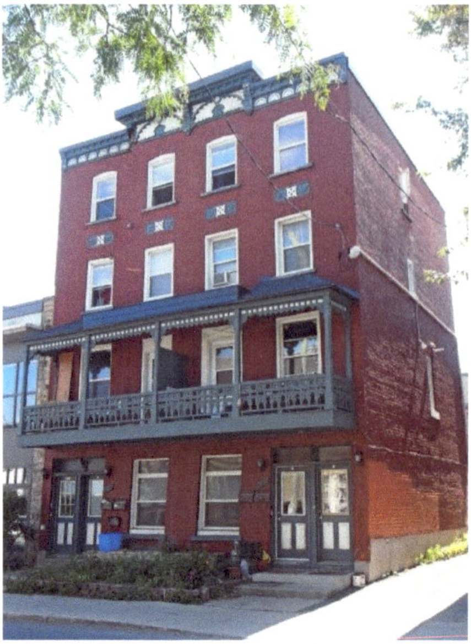
224-226 St. Patrick Street - decorative cornice

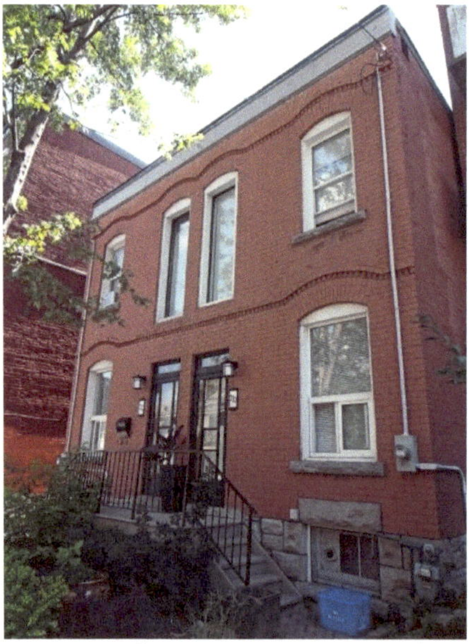
220-222 St. Patrick Street - saw tooth moulding

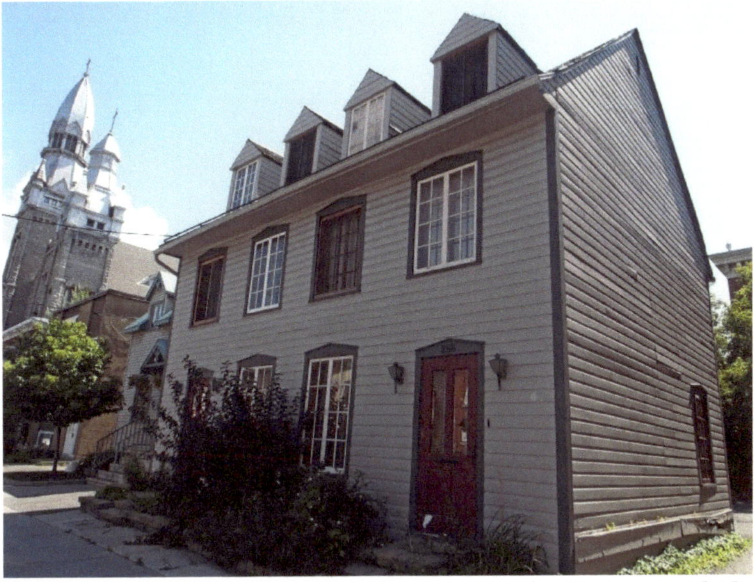

288-290 St. Patrick Street - Thomas Brulé House - 1842 - dormers in attic

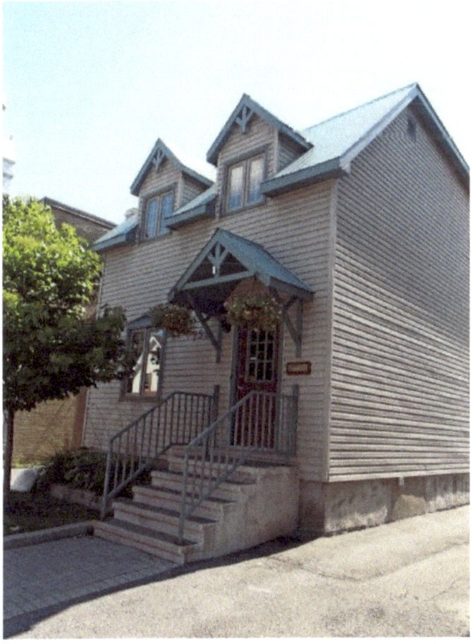

292 St. Patrick Street - gabled dormers with decorative trim

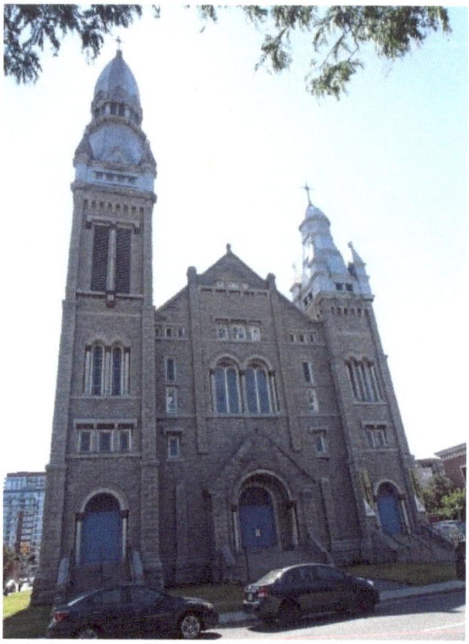

314 St. Patrick Street - Saint Brigid's Centre for the Arts is a multidisciplinary venue for all kinds of artistic, cultural and social events. The center is housed in the magnificent spaces of Saint Brigid's Church, a former Irish Catholic church built in 1890 to serve the English-speaking, Catholic population of the area.

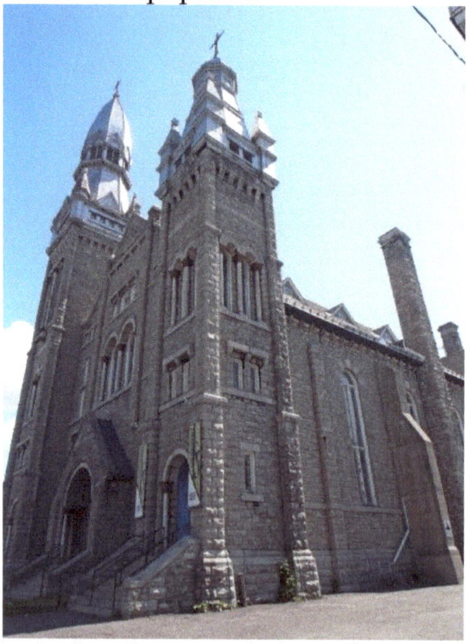

Romanesque Revival style - rounded windows, domes on towers, buttresses

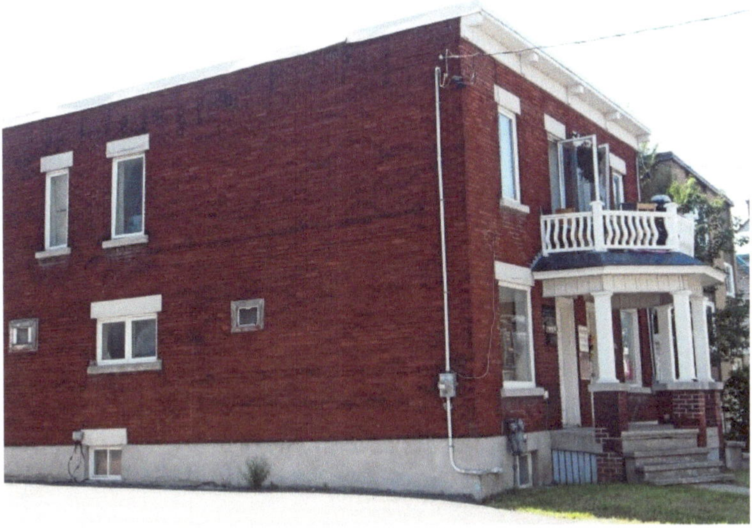

St. Patrick Street – second floor balcony above semi-circular porch

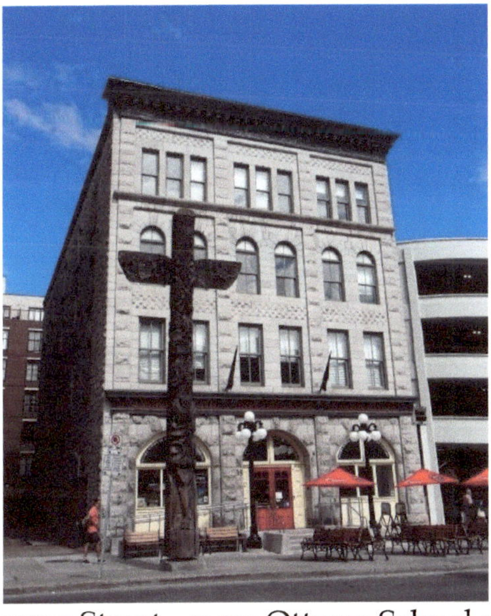

35 George Street – now Ottawa School of Art

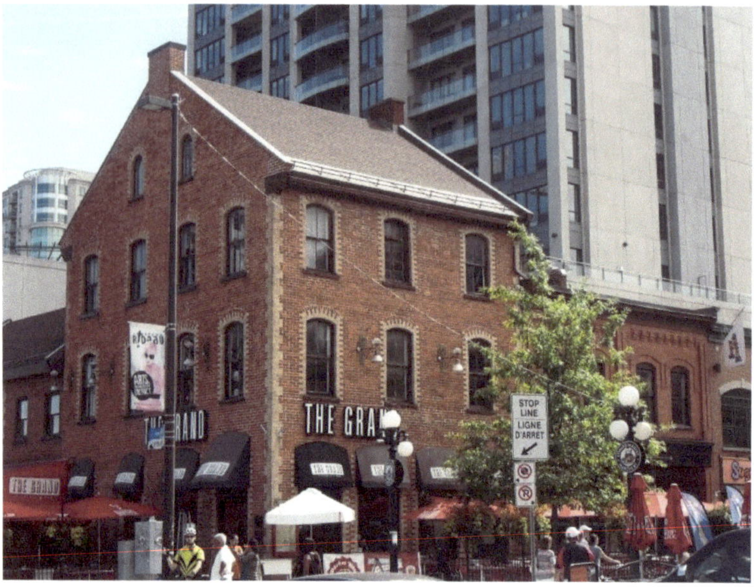

74 George Street - corner quoin, dichromatic brickwork

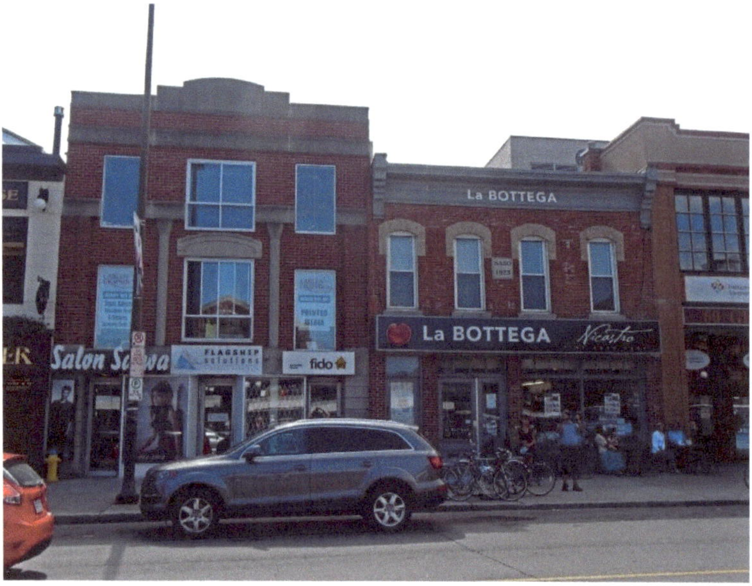

70 George Street - bands, pilasters;
64 George Street - 1923 - La Bottega – voussoirs

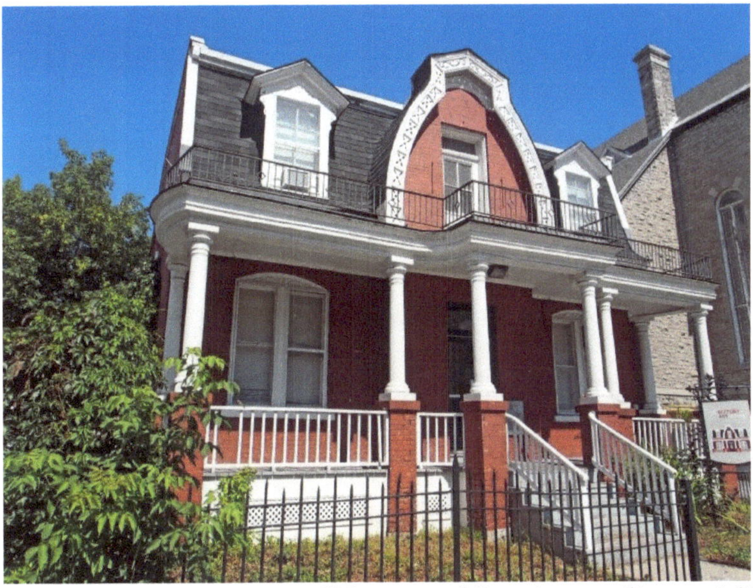

179 Murray Street – a small house of 9 artist studios - aiding the city of Ottawa in developing an artistic and cultural identity – window hoods, Jacobean-type gable, Doric pillars

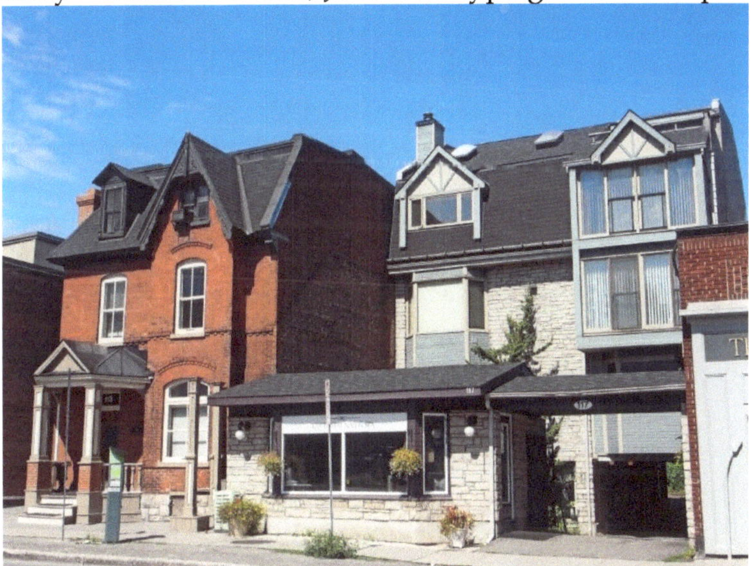

113 Murray Street – saw tooth moulding, pediment, gable and dormer; 117 Murray Street

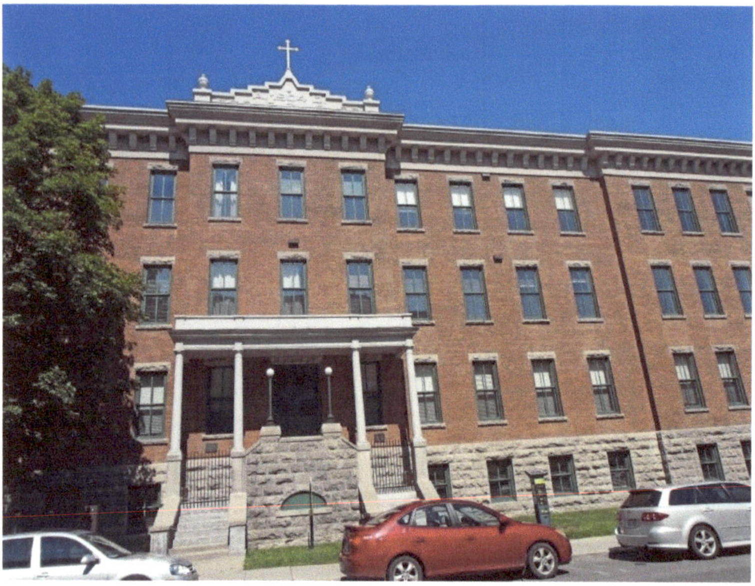

159 Murray Street - Ecole Guigues – The current building opened its doors in 1904 and was one of Ottawa's largest schools. Two sisters, Diane Desloges and Béatrice Desloges, natives of Ottawa and both teachers at the Guigues elementary school, refused to implement the provisions of Regulation 17, thus defying the ministerial order [issued by the Ontario Ministry of Education] that limited teaching in French to the first two years of elementary school. On January 5, 1916, the Ottawa Separate School Board, with nineteen mothers and the Desloges sisters, stormed the entrance of this school to demand that Franco-Ontarian pupils be educated in their mother tongue. It was not until 1927 that bilingual schools in the province were officially recognized.

Thousands of students passed through its halls until it closed in 1979.

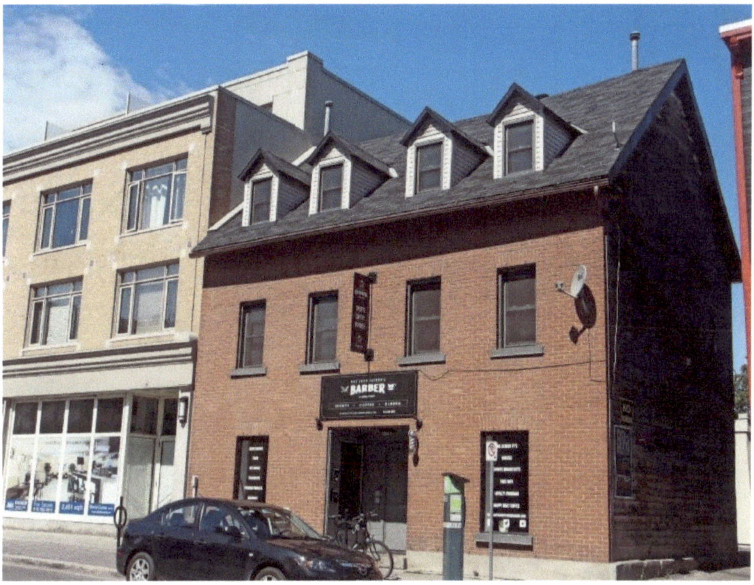

89-91 Murray Street – 1876 - Not Your Father's Barber – dormers in attic

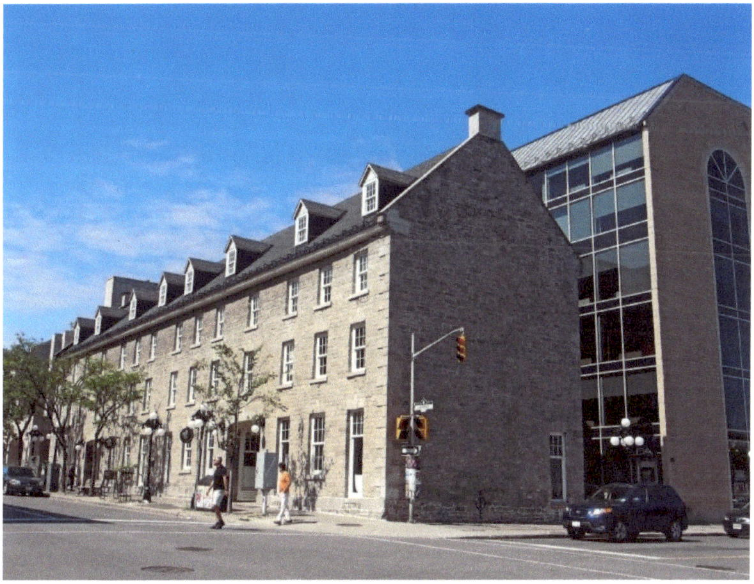
Murray Street – three-storey stone building with dormers

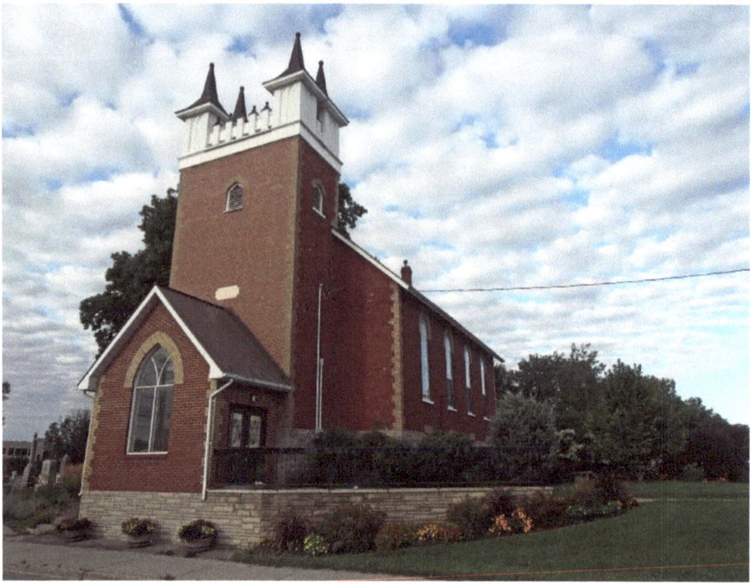

1876 Merivale Road, Nepean - Merivale United Church - built 1875-1876 – Gothic Revival – finials on tower with balustrade; corner quoins

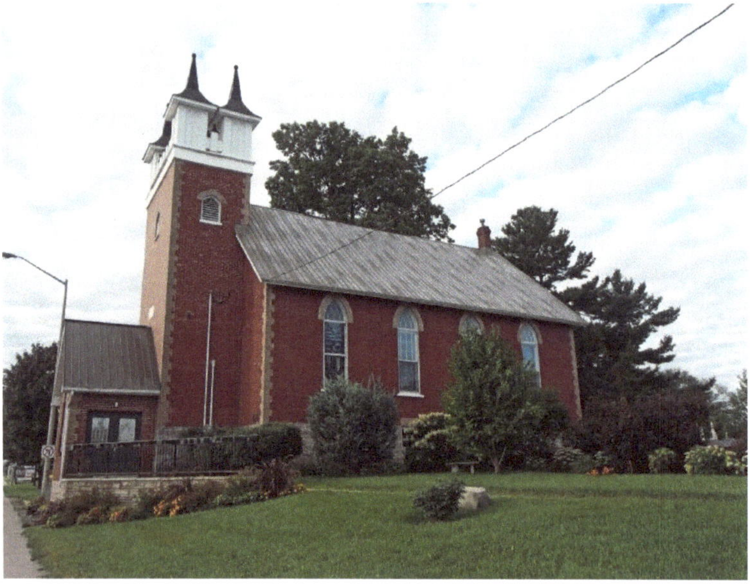

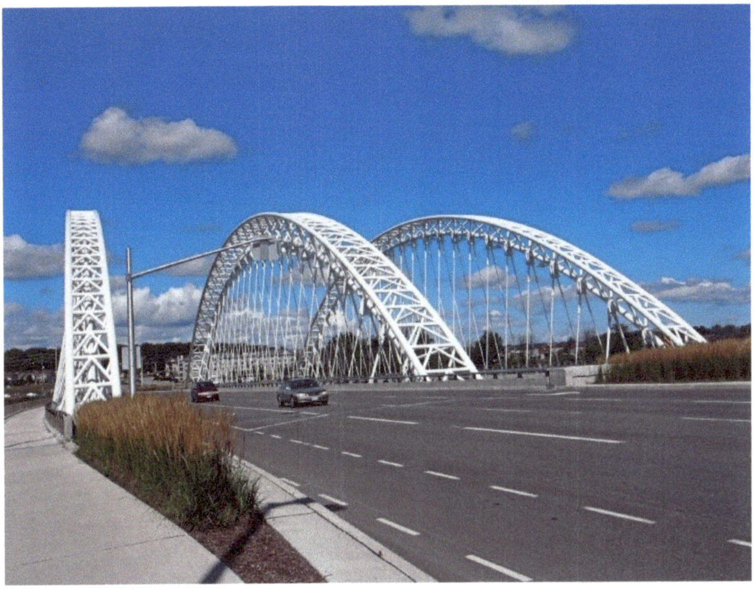

Beautiful bridge

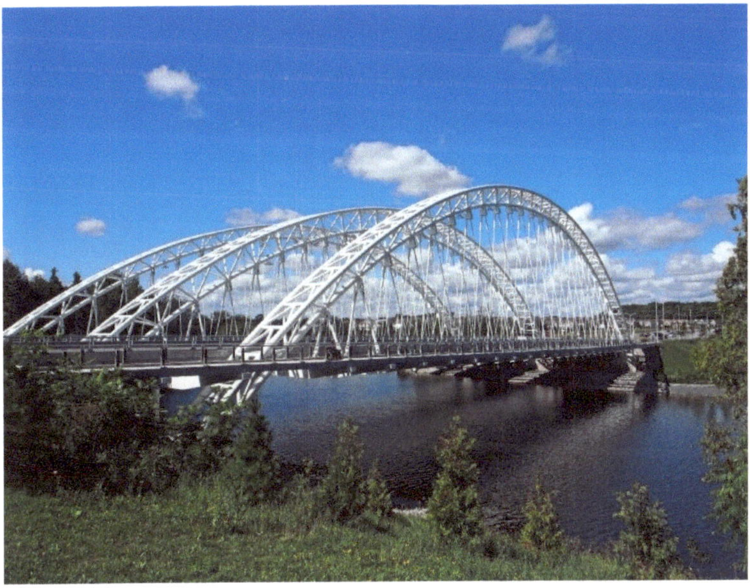

Architectural Terms

Banding: Different materials, colours or textures used in horizontal bands along a wall. Example: 320 Chapel Street, Page 30	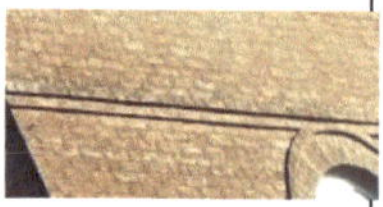
Bay Window: A window that projects out from a wall, in a semicircular, rectangular, or polygonal design. Used frequently in Gothic and Victorian designs. Example: 111 York Street, Page 15	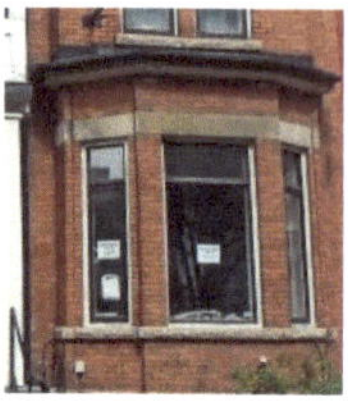
Brackets: a decorative or weight-bearing structural element which forms a right angle with one side against a wall and the other under a projecting surface such as an eave or roof. Example: 18 York Street, Page 10	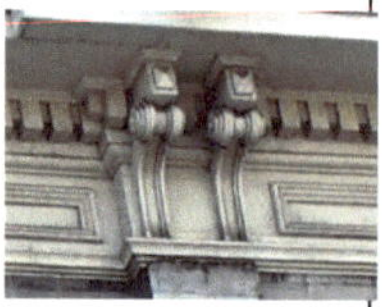
Buttress: a masonry structure built against or projecting from a wall which serves to support or reinforce the wall. In Canadian architecture, they are sometimes used for decoration. Example: 314 St. Patrick Street, Page 45	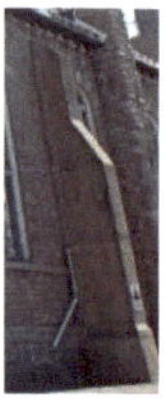

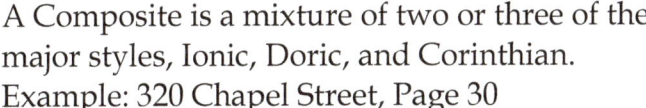

Capital: The uppermost finish or decoration on a column. An Ionic column has a small base, a thin elegant shaft, and a capital composed of volutes which are carved whirls or twists that take the form of a scroll. Example: 312 Laurier Ave. East, Page 24 A Doric column is characterized by a plain column with no base, a shaft with twenty flutings, and a simple capital with a simple entablature. Example: 103 Dalhousie Street, Page 34 A Composite is a mixture of two or three of the major styles, Ionic, Doric, and Corinthian. Example: 320 Chapel Street, Page 30	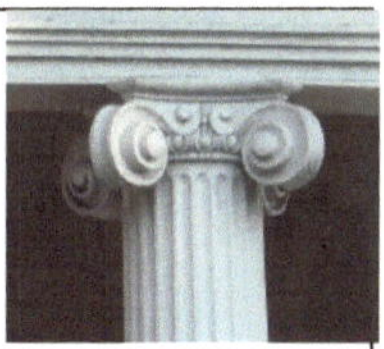 Ionic 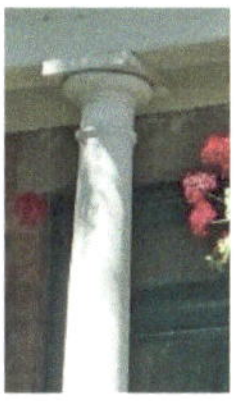 Doric 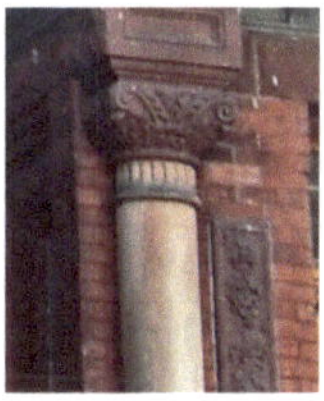 Composite
Cornice: originally the wooden overhang of the roof. With the use of stone, brick, iron and steel, the cornice is any horizontal moulded projection at the top of a building. They can be very decorative. Example: 108 Dalhousie Street, Page 34	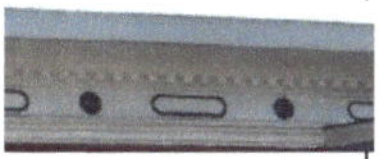
Cornice Return: decorative element on the end of a gable. Example: 88 Dalhousie Street, Page 36	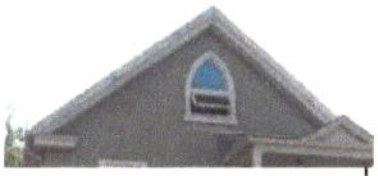
Dentil Moulding: an even series of rectangles used as ornamental decoration in cornices. Example: 50 Byward Market, Page 9	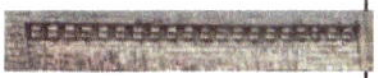

Dichromatic brickwork: the use of two colours of brick, tile or slate to decorate a façade. Example: By Ward Market, Page 8	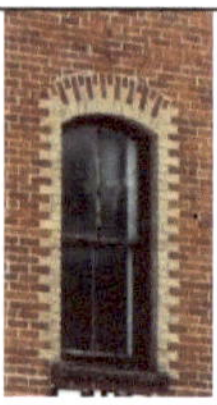
Dome: Any roof structure that is curved and spans an ultimately circular base. Example: 314 St. Patrick Street, Page 45	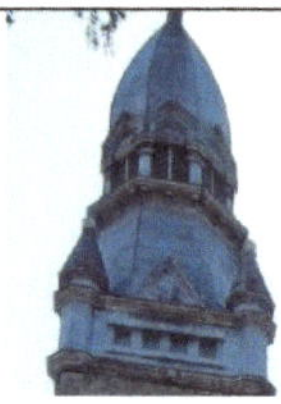
Dormer: (French for "sleep") a gable end window that pierces through the plane of a sloping roof surface to create usable space in the top floor or attic of a building by adding headroom. Example: Chapel Street, Page 31	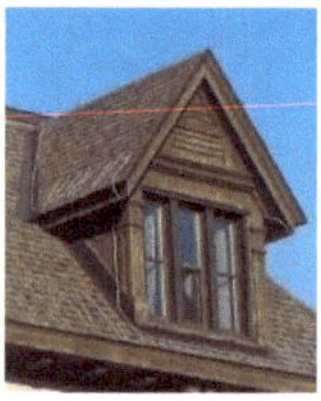
Frontispiece: a portion of the façade of a building, usually a centred doorway that is slightly raised from the rest of the building, usually has extensive ornamentation. Frontispieces are usually Classical in design with white columned porches. Example: Dalhousie Street, Page 35	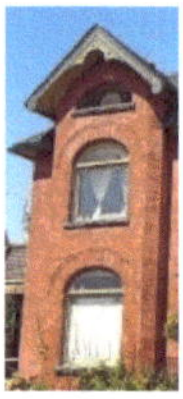
Gable: the triangular portion of a wall between the edges of a sloping roof. Example: 119 York Street, Page 15 **Jacobean Gable:** the gable extends above the roofline. Example: 179 Murray Street, Page 48	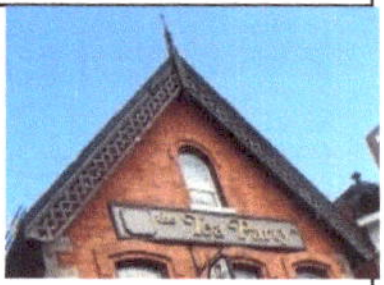 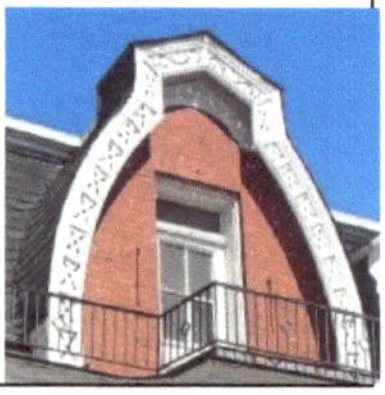

Hipped Roof: a roof where all sides slope downwards to the walls with no gables. Example: Chapel Street, Page 31	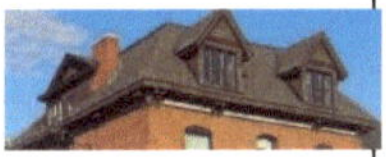
Keystones and Voussoirs: a voussoir is a wedge-shaped element used in building an arch. A keystone is the central stone that locks all the stones into position, allowing the arch to bear weight. A keystone is often enlarged and embellished. Voussoirs: 113-115 Dalhousie Street, Page 33 Keystone: 18 York Street, Page 10	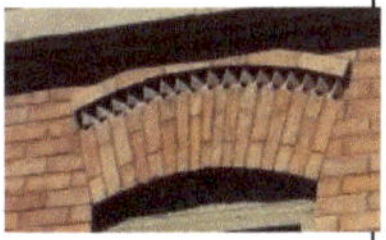 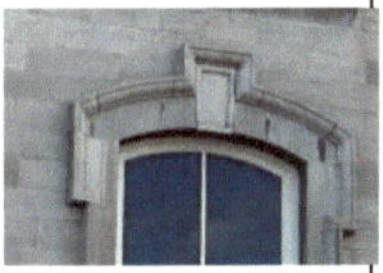
Lancet Window: a tall, narrow window with a pointed arch at its top. Example: 317 Chapel Street, Page 26	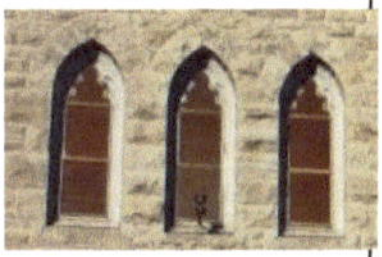
Mansard Roof: This style was popularized by Francois Mansart (1598-1666), an accomplished architect of the French Baroque period and especially fashionable during the Second French Empire (1852-1870). This roof is almost flat on the top section, with two slopes on each of its sides with the lower slope at a steeper angle than the upper and having dormer windows. Example: 323 Chapel Street, Page 32	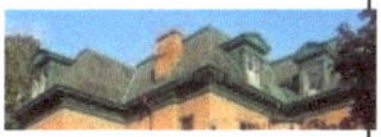
Pediment: a triangular section above the door or portico, usually supported by columns. The inside of the triangle is called the tympanum. Example: 159 Guigues Street, Page 39	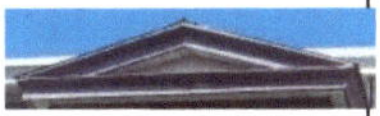

Pilaster: a slightly projecting column built into or applied to the face of a wall for additional structural support. Example: Byward Market, Page 9	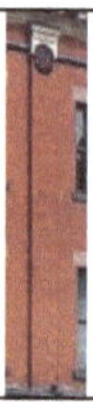
Quoin: masonry blocks at the corner of a wall, often a decorative feature, usually larger or of a different colour than the rest of the wall. Example: 42 York Street, Page 12	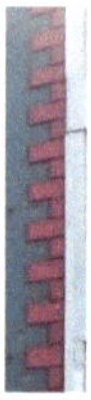
Sidelight: a vertical window that flanks a door, and is often used to emphasize the importance of a primary entrance. **Transom Window:** the light above the doorway, also called a fanlight. Example: 71 Thomas Street, Page 19	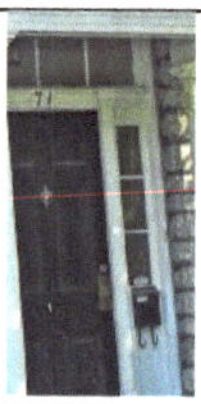
Turret: a small tower that projects from the wall of a building. Example: Dalhousie Street, Page 35	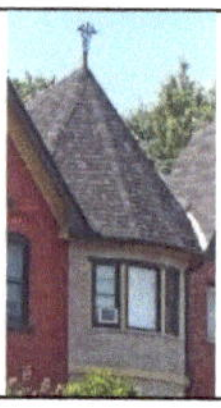
Verge board and Finial: also called bargeboards - hang from the projecting end of a roof and are often elaborately carved and ornamented. **Finial:** ornament added to the top of a gable, pinnacle, canopy or spire - a Gothic element. Example: 127 York Street, Page 18	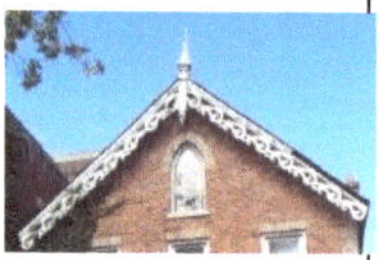
Window Hood: A **hood** is the piece found above window openings, usually of an ornate design, and covers the top third of the opening. Hoods are commonly placed above arched or curved openings on both windows and doors. Example: 179 Murray Street, Page 48	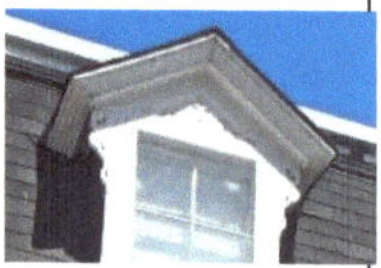

Building Styles

Gothic Revival, 1830-1890 – These decorative buildings have sharply-pitched gables with highly detailed verge boards, pointed-arch window openings, and dichromatic brickwork. It is a common style in Ontario. Example: 62 Somerset Street East, Page 19	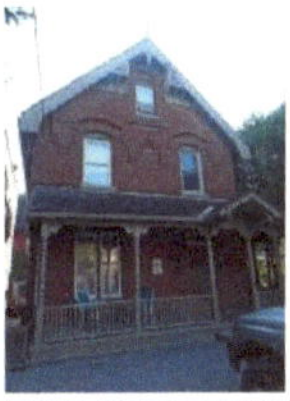
Italianate, 1850-1900 – A two story rectangular building with a mild hip roof, a projecting frontispiece, and generous eaves with ornate cornice brackets was the basis of the style; often there are large sash windows, quoins, ornate detailing on the windows, belvederes and wraparound verandahs. Italianate commercial buildings often have cast iron cresting and elegant window surrounds. Example: 46-48 Somerset Street East, Page 20	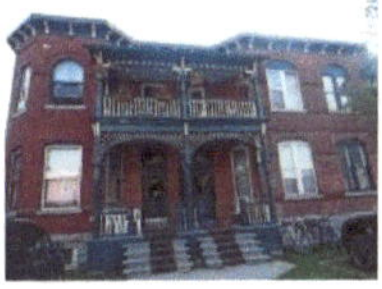
A **log cabin**, built from logs, was usually one- or 1½-storeys constructed with round rather than hewn, or hand-worked, logs, and erected quickly for frontier shelter. Log cabins were built from logs laid horizontally and interlocked on the ends with notches. The cabin was situated to provide sunlight and drainage so the pioneers could cope better with the rigors of frontier life. The pioneers chose old-growth trees that were straight and had few knots and did not need to be hewn to fit well together. Careful notching minimized the size of the gap between the logs and reduced the amount of chinking with sticks and rocks or daubing with mud to fill the gap. Example: 158-160 Guigues Street, Page 38	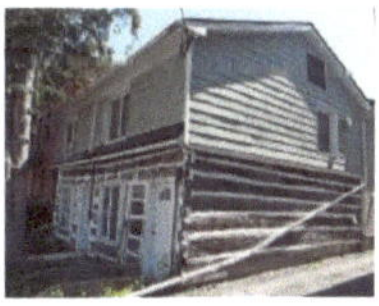

Second Empire, 1860-1880 – The mansard roof is the most noteworthy feature of this style and is evidence of the French origins. Projecting central towers and one or two-storey bays can also be present. Example: 323 Chapel Street, Page 32	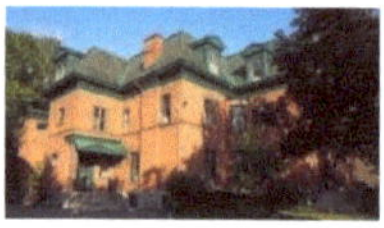
Victorian - In Ontario, a Victorian style building can be seen as any building built between 1840 and 1900 that doesn't fit into any of the other categories. It encompasses a large group of buildings constructed in brick, stone, and timber, using an eclectic mixture of Classical and Gothic motifs. Example: 312 Laurier Avenue East, Page 25	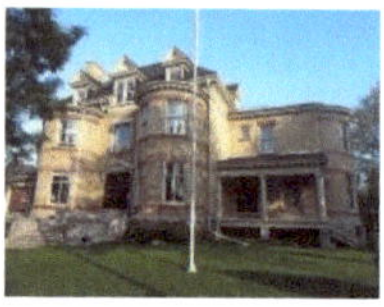

www.ingramcontent.com/pod-product-compliance
Lightning Source LLC
Chambersburg PA
CBHW040852180526
45159CB00001B/404
* 9 7 8 1 5 3 9 1 6 5 0 8 8 *